In the Garden

MARJORIE HARRIS

In the Garden

Thoughts on Changing Seasons

HarperCollins*Publishers*Ltd

IN THE GARDEN: THOUGHTS ON CHANGING SEASONS. Copyright ©
1995 by Marjorie Harris. All rights reserved. No part of this book may be used
or reproduced in any manner whatsoever without prior written permission
except in the case of brief quotations embodied in reviews. For information
address HarperCollins Publishers Ltd, Suite 2900, Hazelton Lanes, 55 Avenue
Road, Toronto, Canada M5R 3L2.

First edition

Canadian Cataloguing in Publication Data

Harris, Marjorie
  In the garden : thoughts on changing seasons

ISBN 0-00-255410-0

1. Gardening.   I. Title.

SB455.H37 1995   635   C95-931374-5

95 96 97 98 99 ❖ HC 10 9 8 7 6 5 4 3 2 1

Printed on 20% recycled paper

Printed and bound in the United States

For Nick

Introduction

Nothing prepared me for gardening except the sheer good luck of having parents and teachers who instilled in me a huge curiosity about anything to do with nature. When we lived in Labrador, one of those wonderful teachers made me gather every plant I could possibly find and then made me learn to identify them. This exercise taught me to love the extraordinary bounty of those opulent few weeks of spring and summer.

My parents' experiments with gardens were always on a grand scale. So grand they could never keep them under control. We would live off the land. They read *The Egg and I*, Betty Macdonald's book about raising chickens. We raised chickens. That year the living off the land and having chickens clashed when all the chickens managed to escape from their pens and dig up every seed that had been so laboriously planted. Since we moved constantly, the huge gardens that were planted never seemed to be in the family long enough to actually harvest a crop. But we did grow vegetables. Valiantly. And I did learn how to prepare soil, sow seeds, hoe, and weed.

When my husband Jack and I bought our own home in 1967, it was an important year for my soul. This was my very own territory, the first I'd ever possessed. My own patch of the yard was almost all vegetables. Until the fateful year when nothing came up. I simply hadn't observed how big the neighbor's weeping willow had grown and how shady the garden was becoming. The garden taught me how to see more clearly.

Having flowers was considered an extravagance by my family and as a consequence I thought so too. But I had to grow something, so flowers it was. And the garden taught me how to experiment.

When children needed the space, they got it. When tenants took over part of the house, the garden was theirs. Finally in the 1980s it was all mine once again: all nineteen by one hundred feet. And I needed every square inch, because, by then, I'd become obsessed about plants.

For many of us, especially we who live in cities, a garden is the only contact with nature and our best source for understanding our relationship with the land. The mere act of putting in a border connects with this history.

Like most gardeners, I get my best ideas when I'm walking or working outside, never when I'm actually near paper or pen. Sometimes an idea will go round and round my mind each time I come to the same place. If I don't set it down, it will continue to nag until I do, otherwise I just keep on writing and rewriting in my head. And surely that way lies madness.

From the very beginning, when we moved here, I've kept notebooks of random thoughts. Sometimes these turned up in newspaper columns, magazine pieces, or in books. Some of those thoughts are now here.

For the last few years, we've been lucky enough to be able to go to the south of France for a month during the winter. This journey has expanded my passion for nature as well as creating an atmosphere that's wonderful for personal musings.

I've assembled these thoughts in no particular order except by season, which seems the logical thing to do as a gardener. And so I share my life with you.

Toronto, 1995

Acknowledgments

Profound thanks to Robert Fulford for reading part of the manuscript and making invaluable suggestions. To Geraldine Sherman who also read part of it and came up with great ideas for entries. To Charlotte Sykes who read the whole manuscript. To Mary Jo Leddy who loaned me so many wonderful books when I started working on this project. To Sheree Lee Olson whose bookshelves were also raided. To my husband, Jack Batten, who had to live through months of writing in a highly charged emotional atmosphere and didn't crumple. To Iris Tupholme who was constantly encouraging, who put things in order, and who did such a good job of editing. To Claude Primeau who thought up this book; and Maya Mavjee who is always helpful. And to Nicholas Shiloh Olson Harris who's brought such complete joy into our lives.

Autumn

Ripeness

Autumn defines ripeness. People think of spring as the beginning of life but that rhythm is, for me, in the autumn. It's my birthday. It's the start of the school year. All around there is an explosion of color, scent, tastes. New beginnings.

I plant bulbs and shrubs. I move things around to make bold arrangements of color, form, and shape. I observe the angle of the hard sun on the plants, making them stretch out poetically.

Everywhere the berries burst from their skins. And harvesting by birds makes the garden vibrate with their ecstatic songs. Some of the berries turn, making the birds flap about drunkenly, dizzy on nature's wine.

I began this garden in September decades ago, and my love for a season is now apparent. I planted things that flower in autumn: masses of chrysanthemums in pale yellows, pinks and white; goldenrod in some form is allowed to stay and flower, moving about the garden at its own will, not mine. There are asters of every imaginable shade, size, and petal form.

I want this to be the richest, most satisfying time for the garden. If I draw enough sensual satisfaction from the autumn months, it will somehow help transport me over the long distances of winter and right into spring. So I cram myself with sensation and color and most years I do pretty well at convincing myself this is a beginning not an ending of the year.

Autumn cleanup

The place is a mess. Huge winds have taken down endless small branches from the willow next door, leaves are fleeing the tree by the millions. Or so it seems. The temptation is to clean everything up. Make it look neat again.

Gardening is not like housekeeping where a little sweeping can improve things. Yet, in gardening a very little tidying goes a long way. You have to think like a forest when you garden. No little elves rush about tidying the forest floor. Fallen leaves lie and slowly break down into the magnificent duff that feeds the trees — providing both a mulch for protection and food for the thriving life in the soil below.

Scraping the ground clean is a big mistake. Leaves return most of the nutrients crucial to soil health. With a really good supply of leaves, it might not be necessary to add anything else to a small garden.

It's impossible to have too many leaves since every one can and should be reused. For years, before they selfishly started keeping them, I used to throw half the neighborhood's leaves onto soil once hidden under a bed of concrete. The soil was sterile — not a worm turning anywhere.

My son, Chris, and I would dig holes, throw the wet leaves in and cover them up. It took three years before the place was filled with worms. They did all the real work in restoring the soil. Now it's smothered in plants. Nature really does look after itself, if we could just learn to leave it alone.

Energy

Why is it that crawling about on the earth can change the shape of a whole day? There are times when all the energy has gone out of my body, I feel flat and vaguely miserable. That's when I go out to the garden. Especially if I'm particularly downhearted. It's where I can remove myself from my Self.

People often say that they get their best ideas when they are weeding, or mowing or doing some kind of garden work. And I think that's because the garden distracts us from looking inward, from being egocentric, self-absorbed. You move from thinker to tinkerer, and free up the more creative side of the brain.

We get this lift from the kind of energy that plants manifest. They radiate it from every inch of the garden — high and low. Just stand by a shrub for twenty minutes and feel what it emanates. Then multiply that by hundreds of plants and you understand why it is we need this little hit of the natural world for revival.

The same sort of thing happens on a much larger scale when we feel the need go to a park or just get away from the city — an increasingly difficult activity.

We've taught ourselves to believe that the earth is infinitely forgiving. So we assault it, batter it and expect it not to fade away or die. But what if? What if all that energy was removed? That we finally achieved the developer's ultimate dream that everything should be exploited and covered and lived on and used for profit? What would be left? Nothing to revive the flagging spirits and probably not a place worth living in.

Nature in the raw

There are not many crows in our neighborhood, so when they kick up a fuss it calls for close attention. I was quietly working away when I heard the crows crying out with what sounded like ferocious anger.

I could see them circling a tree two gardens over. Going to the very back I saw what was troubling them: a huge hawk with a dead squirrel hanging from its beak. The body was limp and bleeding, the hawk implacable.

I'm not enough of a birder to know exactly what kind of a hawk, but if I ever saw a picture I'd recognize this one. It was a beauty. Serene, in spite of the surrounding pandemonium, sure of its prize.

The crows kept up the ruckus. They swooped and dived excitedly into the hawk's tree. I was, of course, cheering for the hawk: one less squirrel to deal with and a decent meal for him.

Tennyson's "Nature red in tooth and claw" accurately described the attitude of most Victorians towards the natural world. It was savage, uncivilized, to be defeated, controlled, subdued — a concept we've never escaped. We see aggressiveness among animals but no poetry. We see competition but no sharing, though we admire these qualities in ourselves. Watching the majestic hawk conjure up the strength to move off on slow spiralling flight to a place where he could eat in peace, I was filled with gratitude. Even in the city these dramatic events come to remind us how close we are to the rawness of nature.

Training to be a gardener

I'm often asked where I got my garden education. The automatic answer is, "In the garden, of course." But that's not good enough for some people. If you don't have certification, how can you possibly be educated? My degree is in English but that didn't necessarily help me become a gardener. It made me love books, which is far more important.

I know some horticultural professionals who have plenty of training and almost no feeling for plants, and others who've never developed an aesthetic towards gardening.

One of the finest gardeners I know has degrees in economics though none in gardening. Yet he is the one person whose garden information I trust implicitly. He can read. He can dig out information and analyze it. And he can apply this to his practises in the garden because he's smart.

The gardeners I spend most of my time with aren't highly trained. They came to it because they loved growing things or couldn't keep their hands off an empty space. They probably continued because they grow things well, or discovered an innate sense of good design. And they do it all themselves. No hired hands for them.

I don't know one who'd miss a seminar, a lecture, or a chance to hit the libraries. They are voracious for information. I know few professional gardeners who have time for this. We have an old saying in our family: Always leave things better than you found them. That's what real gardeners do — trained or untrained.

Leaves

I compost every leaf I can find. I sneak about various neighborhoods collecting other people's leaves and it's usually the wealthier areas where you can pick up the most. Maybe they have more trees than the rest of us, more likely they are just tidier (or have gardeners whose job it is to clean up every wanton leaf). I store them along the side of the house, packed solid in big bags, with just a little soil and moisture added, then I throw them on the compost one by one all winter long. And, if I've been really conscientious in my gathering, through the following year.

I remember the burning of leaves as *the* fall ritual. We scattered the ashes around the garden. Burning was outlawed here at least thirty years ago, yet this is one of the strongest scent-memories I have of childhood.

We stopped burning leaves because it was too dangerous in a jam-packed city. But if we'd known enough, we'd have stopped burning simply because they give us even more back by letting them compost and then putting them back into the garden to keep it well fed and fluffy.

I do rake the paths and stone to give the place just an aura that the controlling hand has passed lightly over the garden. It makes me feel good and it makes autumn a time when there is little garden stress. "You must be so busy at this time of year," people say, but I barely notice if I am.

The air is refreshing and it's fun to be among leaves, checking out the fine tracery patterns and the glorious colors that make this the flashiest time of the year.

Berries

I usually plant shrubs because of the berries they produce. I thought I was choosing them for me, and at first I was. They are a designer's bit of magic. They have blossoms, the fruits arrive giving them another burst of color, and more interest. There are different berries for different seasons as well.

But this didn't occur when I put in the dogwood, the serviceberry, the elder, and some of the roses. Although, they are wonderful plants in themselves. They are here because they can take the shade this garden offers so profusely.

What I didn't think about was the actual function of those berries. Why and when do they appear and for what reason? Berries may be a treat for us, but they are critical to the animals who depend on them for survival. They are lures that say "Eat me" so that their seeds can be passed on and replanted. I didn't know that Virginia creeper turns bright red to announce their berries to birds heading south for the winter.

If I had known what I was doing, of course I'd have chosen all the same shrubs. Some berries ripen in the height of summer, others come along in fall, and the most difficult ones to digest hang on until desperate winter days when birds will eat anything including the dreaded bittersweet which lives up to its name.

These autumn splendors are now imbued with yet another subtle layer of meaning in the garden.

The larger context

Most of us think about our own little garden space as an earthly paradise over which we have complete control. We can do anything we want here, a stark contrast to the rest of life. But thinking about gardens in a larger context is to understand a garden's *genius loci*.

This means analyzing what the landscape has to offer rather than imposing upon it something we've seen in a garden book or somewhere else. It's understanding how to work with nature and how to give this place a sensible, solid basis, reflected in the changing season. It comes from an understanding of how we are connected to everything around us.

Our garden plots are part of a complex system that animals have come to depend on in the city. By animals, I mean all sorts of insects as well as the fur-bearing kinds. If a garden is designed to attract birds, butterflies, moths — if it has thickets (or hedgerows of shrubs with lots of fruits), this will provide a place for many of these animals to live in. There has to be water since all wildlife must have water to survive. And they need lots of different families of native plants. It means knowing and adjusting to the environment.

It's going back to the way we were before we could use earth-moving equipment to take the top off hills if they were inconvenient to us. It means becoming sensitive to everything around us and not just our own wants.

Stoning the garden

Stones are everywhere — on front lawns, strewn over paths. They make rivers, streams, waterfalls and ersatz mountains, cliffs and bays. Rocks are being ripped out of fields, looted from the edges of lakes and anyone owning shares in a quarry must be making a lot of money.

I thought, at first, that this business of putting a great huge rock in the middle of the lawn was an urge to return to the primal Shield, the original rock, the mythopoetic past. I fear it's just another trendy garden craze of rock heaped or scattered about.

One of the major reasons for stoning the environment is that it produces instant results. The well-stoned garden doesn't require much maintenance. Weeds certainly can't get past these barriers and they do a good job of keeping things clean and warm. But what a sight it is to see this kind of overkill. Backhoes and forklifts are needed to get them into place.

I am not an anti-rock or stone person. One time we were on a trip to Oregon and my husband tried to lift my suitcase. "Is this thing full of rocks?" he asked. Of course it was, just a few mementoes of every beach we'd visited. I became a rockhound overnight. I took my collection of stones and made little designs hidden around shrubs and through the garden.

I love the idea of adding anything that gives the garden texture, evokes a memory or two, and looks pretty in its place. But beware the stoned garden, it can become a dead place.

A rose garden

I never wanted a rose garden. Traditional planting seems too stiff and regimented for my blowzy taste. Having a few dozen fussy hybrid tea roses lined up in rows, always ready for picking, takes up too much room. I want the color all over the place, not only in a concentrated patch.

I don't know when this habit of planting roses in rows started. It was probably in English gardens where the rose is revered above all other plants. To my eye, those long legs look bare and unappealing no matter what kind of a garden.

I immediately want to cover them up or let a clematis or sweet pea vine run rampant through them, providing some modesty, making them seem less, well, like a clutch of nudes caught *in flagrante*.

I adore roses and have lots of them in the garden. But they get no special area and must live with everything else I love as well. I prefer the old roses, the ones that haven't been improved, that haven't lost their endearing scent or turned into a weird bluish color. These ancient roses carry with them the weight of history — the bourbons, the damascenes, the moss — for an added bit of enchantment and mood.

Time

Time is a difficult element for anyone to grapple with. But it's even more so for the gardener. You constantly look at a garden and compare it to what it was like a few weeks ago. You spend a good deal of time imagining what it will look like in a few years.

Pascal writes, "We never keep to the present. We recall the past; we anticipate the future as if we found it too slow in coming and were trying to hurry it up, or we recall the past as if to stay its too rapid flight." Gardeners can appreciate that.

But the garden does have a way of dragging us into the present. You stop to spend hours gazing on a blossom. Who knows when this moment will come again? Perhaps not for another year.

Time is more fleeting in the garden than elsewhere, I think. You can be in the garden for no more than a few minutes, and two hours have passed.

This of course runs at odds with how the world works. You don't just give up hours and hours and hours on a hobby. Not that any serious gardener sees this as a hobby. Non-gardeners are amazed when I mention how much time I spend in the garden. How can you possibly garden eight hours a day and still work? Easy — you get up earlier, you work later, and you don't do lunch. I picked up two hours a day when I stopped smoking.

I used to see my friends at noon. Now, I'm in the garden. Time has shifted its grip on my life. Now, I can ignore it.

The weeping mulberry

I can't remember why I bought the weeping mulberry. Along with a serviceberry, a burning bush, and a Japanese sandcherry, it was the first of dozens of shrubs I planted. They were ordinary plants though I didn't know that at the time. I liked the shape, the way they looked, and that the bark in each was completely distinctive. They live on, except the sandcherry. It was cut down but I don't remember when, it was so long ago.

The other day a stranger to the garden said, "Why don't you get that mulberry out of here. You'll be able to see the rest of the garden so much better." I was shocked. I hate anyone making suggestions about *my* garden (though I'm generous with my own ideas on other gardens). It would never occur to me to even move that plant.

This mulberry has gone through several transformations. It used to droop right down to the ground for the kids to use as a hideout or to rest from the sun. Then the cat took it over as a cool retreat. Later I got quite fancy and lopped it into a standard with growth only at the top. Lots of light can get through to the plants around.

The little tree produces fruit that birds and squirrels adore. It has a kind of gnarled elegance which symbolizes the aging of the garden. It's so much more important to maintain all that history than to see the lines of the berm, or let sunlight fall on the path behind. The mulberry stays with us for the rest of its life. And the life of this garden.

Wasp's nest

The wasp's nest was an incredible surprise. It was so delicate and wondrously intricate, but hidden among the leaves of a neighbor's Katsura tree. The big heart-shaped leaves made the ideal screen. Once the leaves had fallen, this fragile bit of perfection became exposed: a sac made up of what looked like crumpled silk.

Ever since then, I've been looking for wasp's nests because of their magnificence. I've seen an artisan who collects them and then shapes them into shades for candles. They are magical, and if I had the money, I'd own one.

Wasps abandon these fragments of beauty once the cold weather sets in. They lay their eggs in nests which can be found almost anywhere from logs to the window of a house. When they go their own way in the fall the queen hibernates in the bark of a tree and will form another colony in the spring.

Wasps fulfill many functions, but one of the most interesting, the braconid wasps, have tiny wormy larvae that feed on caterpillars and aphids by overwintering in the host. Comes spring and, bingo, death.

I have never been afraid of wasps until recently when, after twenty-seven years in this garden, I was finally bitten by one. As I was stirring up the compost, a tiny wasp flew up and bit me right under the eye. My husband said I looked like Jake La Motta after a bad bout. I'm more wary now and that makes me a bit sad. I want all of nature to be my friend.

Water in the garden

Have you ever asked yourself where squirrels, bees, butterflies, and all the other animal life get a drink of water? They must have some to stay alive. Observe. They'll take it where they can get it and in whatever condition. An old pot left outside with some soil and rainwater in it is more of a home to these animals than the cute little birdbath that developed a crack and never held water after the first winter.

I became very concerned about water when I left a big metal bowl outside for the cat and found every bug in the place attracted to it because they were so parched.

Watching a bee take dainty stabs at sipping some water is good enough entertainment on a hot summer afternoon. The landing field is too slippery but this huge insect goes at it again and again.

The raccoons make no bones about how much *they* like water. A fresh bowl set out for them at night is filthy by morning. They've brought in whatever food they found to be cleaned.

One summer night, the raccoons completely trashed my carefully wrought little water garden. The fountain with plants had been there for weeks and they'd ignored it. This night they tore the plants out of the water, examined them carefully, threw them all over the deck and then shambled off. Now the decision is whether to replace the plants, or attract them elsewhere so they'll leave the fountain alone. Sometimes trying to live cooperatively with nature in the city can be complicated.

Death of a friend

When I heard about this death, it was a shock because my friend was so young. There seems no reason for him to die. No excessive living. No disease that anyone knew of and yet he isn't here now. The garden reflects the gloomy mood this death has brought on. The leaves are listless and brown as they sit unstirring on the ground. There is no sun.

Everywhere around me this November day seems to speak of ends: of life, of season, of joy. Nature is supposed to be doing its job today. It's supposed to be making me think of renewal, respite from mourning, distract me by its beauty. But I find no solace here. No comfort.

Rakes and gloves had been dropped helter-skelter. Baskets of compost lie untended and the screening unfinished. Piles of twigs are scattered about waiting to be bundled up. A box of tulips is still waiting to be planted and it feels like it's too late, too cold now. And I've lost my will to plant.

I spend an hour sitting on the bench, thinking about the influence he'd had on my life, my work, and what a crazy joyous person he was. Did I ever tell him that? Probably not.

After a long meditation on his life, I start thinking about his death. The sun is trying to break through the clouds and a little warmth has come into the air. In a desultory way, I start to pick things up. One thing leads to another and before I know it I'm blending the thoughts of death into the need to do something with the mess. We carry on.

Privacy

To be alone in the garden, it's necessary to wrap ourselves inside an invisible cloak of privacy. I don't know how this unspoken rule works when we're so jammed together in the middle of the city, but it does.

There are days when it's the best thing in the world to lean over the fence and have a long chat with a neighbor. Then there are the days when it's unbearable to speak to anyone.

No one discusses this kind of mood. It's sensed. You want to go outside but you want to be alone. Maybe it's just primary instinct for survival in close quarters. Animals surely have it when they drone away in hives, or are part of a warren. Or is it just people who actually need privacy?

I can get a certain kind of privacy going into my own thoughts, daydreaming, or making things up to get through crowded city streets. But I don't think of that as being in a cloak of privacy — which is quite special and observable.

To be private, it isn't necessary to be alone. But there are times when only aloneness will do. I can get peopled-out pretty quickly. Their energy is suddenly draining, so when I go into the garden to be alone, it's also to get recharged.

I guess this is why I like to be in the garden after dark. I can sit on a bench and be perfectly still, and have all the privacy I want.

Moonlight

When we sit out on the deck in the fading light, the flowers come out to shine. The pale ones, especially the white ones, glow as though by some mysterious inner light. If we stay out long enough, the moonrise moves slowly through the garden, captured in the reflection of a gazing globe, in the mirrors set into fences, in the pools of water. Its brilliance surrounds us.

I plant these white flowers to create luminescence at night. Moonlight gives a kind of sheen, a lustre to plants all other lights fail to do. Moths flutter all through the garden on their nightly mission of collecting nectar from those blooms that open only in the dark, especially for them. The strange ipomea or moon vine, nicotine, evening scented stocks — they all glisten with new radiance in the dark. Their scents embrace us.

By the light of the moon, I see bats flying through the garden picking up their nightly supply of mosquitoes and other bugs. I see the cat going through the plants hunting for something whose presence I can feel but can't see.

There are scuttling sounds all through the garden. In my imagination thousands, maybe millions, of bugs are waiting for me to go indoors so they can start their night of chewing away at the tasty banquet proffered.

The squirrels have finished their play, the clear light shows the way to the skunk and the family of raccoons that use the garden during their evening wanderings. There may be rats, but we haven't seen any. Cats make their eerie love songs.

Moonlight becomes a garden most of all.

Bats

The kids didn't tell me for years. As devoted fans of vampire movies, they were sure that I'd be terrified of bats. Then one evening, sitting out on the deck, I saw this silent air force darting overhead, zooming into our garden.

The backyard, a haven of weeds, was just the sort of place bugs like to hang out. The bats were doing their job of eating up to six hundred in an hour. They circle and swoop into seemingly impossible spaces to catch their prey — aided by sonar magic.

I do close the curtains at night and I do hope bats don't get into any tiny little spaces to nest in the house. Years ago we rented a cottage for a week. During the night I could hear noises and hollered, "Animal inside!" Sure enough it was a bat. We did the traditional thing, which is to flap about with a tennis racquet, scaring the wits out of the beast. Eventually it flew out of the house, confused and terrified.

I didn't like living with a bat at such close quarters. Night after night of batting about makes for a restless sleep. But I don't mind them coming into the garden and keeping it cleaned up. I impressed my kids by not reacting to the bats. They thought I was being something I wasn't. I turned into the usual bore explaining how useful these animals are to us. And that the legends attached to them are just that — some primordial fear of our own that we stick onto another being. They prefer Dracula.

Good neighbors

A good neighbor spoils you for all others. We've had only two neighbors on each side. It's a steady, solid place to live. In each case, a disagreeable neighbor was replaced by someone amiable.

What an extraordinary difference. With mean neighbors there are days when you don't want to use your garden if they are using theirs. With a good neighbor, you want to share, to make plans to take down the fences. We even tried this on one side. We needed a new fence, we agreed to what it should look like (large open-square lattice) and to leave part of it unfinished so that we could have an airier feel in the garden and planted a living fence of shrubs all along the lot line.

The fence went up and looks very handsome. But the open spaces were soon found wanting. The old dog died and the new one who took her place didn't understand about "living fences." Up went scraggly looking wire barriers, and vines to cover them up were encouraged.

But the sharing goes on. My neighbor says she wants only hardy invasive plants and I give them to her with pleasure. And watch to see her garden grow. As the children get bigger, they use the garden less and less.

It's the cycle of my own family all over again. I know the minute she'll turn into a gardener: she'll turn down my offers and will start collecting things on her own. Until then, what I've got she's welcome to.

Thinking like a forest

W hen you start thinking like a forest, it becomes apparent that you can't run huge machines through your heart, chop down everything in sight, and expect to survive.

The idea that the best tree in the forest should be pulled down to make a boardroom table becomes offensive if you think of that tree as the producer of the very seeds that will ensure the survival of the forest.

Trees are not dead, inanimate objects. They have a complex life that we know very little about. Because they can't get out of the way of danger, they've developed a special way of dealing with all sorts of problems. They are highly compartmentalized and "know" for instance when they are being attacked. By closing down the area under assault, the rest of the tree is protected. Each compartment of a tree is part of a self-supporting, generating system. This means they can take almost any impact by having both living and dead material within this one system. Except those huge inexorable machines — against them there is no possible protection.

When you think about actually culling forests so that many of the greatest trees survive to produce other trees equally strong and healthy, you begin to think of the forest in terms of generations and how good stock makes for better progeny. When you realize how many jobs could be saved if using the latest technology wasn't considered more important than a human being with the skill to harvest a tree humanely, you begin to realize that the forest could be saved and so could jobs.

Smoking in the garden

I admit it, I'm an ex-smoker, the kind everyone hates: I'm now allergic to cigarette smoke which may be real or imagined. I can't remember if I loved to have a cigarette as I drifted through the garden. Now when somebody smokes outside I find it offensive. It masks all the wonderful scents that abound in this place. The plants and I worked hard to make each season as aromatic as possible.

So in comes a visitor extolling the garden's beauties, then as though to underline it — lights up. What can they smell but cigarette? And the smell drifts on the air for what seems like an inordinately long time.

Smokers should be wary of what they touch in the garden. Tobacco is a strong poison, so strong it was once used indiscriminately as a herbicide and a pesticide. Now we just put it in our lungs. If you grow tomato plants, and you smoke, you must wash your hands before you touch the leaves; nicotine on a smoker's hand can harm the delicate plant leaves.

We now force smokers out of doors. But it makes walking the street like dodging cudgels. You never know when they'll light up and put a hole in your new winter coat as they self-absorbedly scuttle along puffing away like guilty creatures.

I don't want to have a huge No Smoking sign hanging over my garden. I would like people to consider this another room in my house. If you can't smoke in my home, please don't smoke in my garden. It's only good manners.

Children in the garden

How could I raise four absolutely wonderful children and not produce a gardener among them? Wasn't I insistent that they help plant seeds? That they could choose any area they wanted for themselves? Theoretically all first-rate rules. But it didn't take somehow.

The garden to them was a wild place. We left some areas untended — good for crawling around and building forts. They made hideaways so secret I didn't know they were going through the fence on to other properties — not done in this area — children could be destructive.

I chose the sunniest part of the garden for myself to grow vegetables. They weren't at all interested in that. And don't believe anything you've heard about radishes. Kids couldn't care less about them. The one thing they did love were scarlet runner beans. This must have been the bean from "Jack and the Beanstalk." It grows at about two feet a day to a length of thirty feet if it has a bit of sun. Then it produces huge heart-shaped leaves, with magnificent scarlet flowers and long edible beans. Very tasty, if you eat them early enough, thin enough.

The first year we planted them and promptly left for a friend's cottage. When we returned two months later, the beans had grown up and over and practically inundated the yard to the absolute delight of all except the crabby next-door neighbor.

I look longingly at the next generation wondering how I can plant the seeds of future passion there. And when my own children will become old enough to need gardening in their own lives.

The garden party

Members of a worthy cause asked me if they could use my garden to do a little fund-raising. How could one say no? I like them all. It's flattering.

A quick survey with the eyes of a stranger and I knew the garden was a mess. Too many holes, not enough color, junk everywhere. For a week, I threw myself into repairs — cursing the whole time. The usual litany — I garden for me, why am I letting strangers come in here? — but I had to admit it did look pretty good when I finished. I disciplined myself not to say, "You should have seen it two weeks ago," or, "It's so much better next month."

I was unbelievably nervous. Not since the children's public school recitals have I been as shaky. I felt my ego, my aesthetics, my sanctuary were on the line. Everyone would find faults. They'd see that I wasn't a very good gardener. I would hate them all.

The day was absolutely glorious. I would lead little groups through the garden, talking knowledgeably about various plants, the theory behind the design. Each person grabbed a glass of wine and lit out into the garden. Soon they were milling about all over the place. What's this plant? (can't remember), why'd you do this? (not sure), what's that? (don't know). At one point there was a dead silence as a hummingbird flashed through heading for a favorite bloom. Suddenly I felt at one with all these lovely people willing to pay money for a good cause to look at my work.

Anthropomorphism

can't help how tacky it sounds but I think of my garden in very human terms. Thus birds "argue" (they of course may only be discussing the weather or where the next meal is coming from). Earthworms "cringe" from my touch (autonomic recoil action to change in temperature?). And plants definitely "look sad."

I quite often refer to plants as "those little guys over there." I hope not to sentimentalize them. According to one wise author, sentimentalizing nature is for the rich and the violent (I can't remember why now). And since I'm neither, I think of this as anthropomorphizing and nothing more.

I didn't always feel this close to my plants. When I started out they were the Other. Something that would or wouldn't grow for me, and I was never sure if I had a green or a brown thumb. Now I see them as little creatures to be handled properly, that have personal likes and dislikes.

Plants feel. Some move their heads with the sun (heliotropism) and others will shut down their blooms as soon as the sun starts going down. Are they resting? Or keeping the night-flying moths out of the blooms?

It requires a lot of time just looking at something which grows at the same rate that paint dries — very, very slowly. But you fall in love with almost anything if you stare at it long enough.

I love my plants. I'll feel passionate about them. But I will never, ever give them names. Some of us know when to draw a line.

Boredom

I get bored. Not often, sometimes when I'm sick of people, not caring about the conversation going on at a party, or stuck somewhere I don't want to be. Then, I get bored.

If you garden, you never get bored. Once you recognize that you are on the cusp of boredom, you think about new plant combinations, when and where you'll put them. This takes up a lot of space in the head.

You do have to be a bit careful not to flip into this ruminative state when you are talking to someone. It's terribly disconcerting to see an old chum, start chatting, and then find your mind adrift because the colors in her scarf are flawless. Would this work in the garden? What plants would be comparable? Threads of conversation fray.

But it's not terrible to cut loose mentally when you are being prodded or poked into a situation you'd rather not be in. It's absolutely all right to spin a new border design in your head.

The difficulty is in remembering it all. If much of gardening is in these flashes of intuition, then you've always got to have a little notebook and pen at the ready. I won't insult you by copying out a profound insight in front of you. I might dissemble a little and say, "What an interesting idea, may I write that down?" Just don't believe everything a gardener tells you; we are very selfish people at times.

Gardening memorabilia

I think of some of the things I've found in the toolshed over the years as collector's items. Take wooden fruit baskets. They were saved for the childrens' school to see which class could collect the most and win some small prize with the recycling money they brought in. No one collects cardboard baskets. I still find the old ones useful for carrying tools around in.

Then there are the tools I absolutely had to have and used only once. An interesting scuffle hoe bought just about the same time I gave up digging. I might find a use for it someday.

The knee guards that will give either varicose veins if they are on too tight, or keep falling down if they aren't on tight enough. I wore them once working in the front garden and had the entire neighborhood in tears of laughter. Even gardeners have a bit of pride.

There's a weird-looking Japanese thing with a wicked-looking curved blade. I guess it's for cultivating. But I don't do that anymore either.

I quite like the gizmo that you can make deep holes with just by twisting it around. I don't know why it's here and not in the compost where it's good for aerating the heap.

Being a garden consumer is something I've tried to get away from not because I'm so pure of heart — I want space so that I can put more stuff in the toolshed.

The earthquake

I hope never to be in an earthquake. The terror must be appalling. I had a small taste. One morning around six, I was lying in bed reading when Mickie, the cat, gave out what could only be described as a bloodcurdling scream. Seconds later the whole house shook. I could see the frames around the big windows move. The whole experience lasted for twenty-seven seconds. I divined what was happening immediately and timed it.

The confusion was evident on the radio — the perfect instrument in an emergency. "What's happening?" the host begged of his audience. The phone calls started to pour in: a parrot had gone completely bonkers; another's bird had fallen off of its perch apparently dead of fright. Dogs and cats everywhere had been scared witless.

This ability of animals to sense something going on deep in the earth has been recorded for thousands of years. We don't take canaries into mines for nothing. But having the earth's natural adjustments come this close to home is terrifying.

The idea of these tectonic plates that make up our planet grumbling a little, let alone shifting, gives us pause to consider our place here. We are so used to being able to control nature, or at least thinking we can control it. When something of this magnitude hits, it should give us some kind of perspective. For a brief moment we realize we are here on the sufferance of nature, because of its bounty. We are not the glory of nature, only one small part of it.

Grace notes

The grace notes of late autumn are evident all over the garden. The silvery gray of the buddleia becomes more intense with each new frost. This radiant plant is a small wonder. At first there is the silver foliage of late spring, then there's the intense blue blossoms that dazzle into late summer. True to its common name, it attracts butterflies.

And the artemisias, always a joy, are pungent with scent right now. A 'Silver king' may get ratty looking as the season changes, but it flops gracefully over stones and other plants in the process of dying, adding a fulsome quality to the scene.

A. 'Powis Castle' looks as regal as ever. Almost shrub-like in its density, filling huge gaps in the waning scene. Even though winter will devastate this plant, it comes back young and refreshed in spring. *A. arborescens* is even more gleaming, and more scented. It stands out now there is little competition for attention.

The *Daphne burkwoodii* remains intact with its pale silver-edged green leaves. And on closer inspection I spy one lonely aromatic bloom struggling to open up before winter. The gorgeous *Ruta graveolens* 'Curly girl' with its ice-blue, deeply cut foliage looks almost like metallic lace.

These grace notes cheer me up and make me look forward to a time next spring when I'll be able to add to this exuberant scene. A gardener is always optimistic.

Winter

The first snow

Y ou can tell as soon as the snow starts to fall that this one will stay. The birds go crazy, arguing over food set out in the neighoring gardens. I have yet to put in a bird feeder. Maybe it's laziness, maybe I don't want to feed the pigeons.

In my own garden, everything has been left alone. It's going to look terrible in the spring, but right now it is wonderful. If this is how birds survived without any help from us, I muse, then there must be some sanity in not cutting down the plants. Let them go to seed for the animals who may need them when foraging gets to be difficult.

I think about the birds becoming dependent on my whims in putting out food — what becomes of them then? When I go away will someone take over? So much responsibility and it isn't even cold yet.

The fences are lined with house finches and the resident blue jays try to scream them into discouragement. Nothing works. They leap about between snowflakes, grabbing at the fruit on the cotoneaster, and the rose hips.

I get to feel fairly chummy with birds at this time of year snug in a warm house. They are out there doing all the work, gathering and feeding — for my amusement. I hate this attitude. So I turn aside and make a cup of cocoa. The first of the season.

Winter creativity

Winter was created for gardeners. We pause now that there's no reason to mess about in the garden. Sleeping plants don't need a controlling hand. Nothing is left to do but to contemplate what comes next.

This respite is the most creative time of the year — when winter fantasies bloom. What to move where? What new plants to get? How to fix up desperately barren spots? Then there's the nagging annual thought — just dig up the whole place and start all over again.

Gardens are like children. "This is my favorite age," I say to my kids. And they reply, "That's what you said last year." Just like a garden. It looks better and better the older it gets. I spend more and more time in admiration. What gleanings are there here? What will it teach me?

I think increasingly about this, especially during the winter months. The mounds under the snow become abstract shapes — I can change them with the wave of a hand. My fantasy life heats up.

But winter is also when everything is seen more clearly. Every error is glaringly obvious. Not enough punctuation with green; and the scarlet of the coralbark maple is almost invisible against the dull gray of the fence, naked without its covering of vines. It needs the frame of a deep green yew to bring out its glories.

Winter is a time for renewal. For plants as well as for gardeners. I try to remember this when I complain about the cold.

Ephemeral snow

It was sunny only a few hours ago, autumn only a few days ago. Now the first snowstorm is screaming out of the northwest backed by arctic winds. For a moment we thought this glorious autumn would never end. We are too soon embraced by winter.

This snow won't last. But it does herald the end of the growing season. I'm suddenly worried about the evergreens. They keep on transpiring all winter and I wonder if they got enough water in the fall. They'll die if they can't draw moisture from the depths of the soil. I've got enough dead plants to contend with so I can't afford to lose one of them. I identify with those plants slowing down into dormancy — asleep beneath the frozen earth.

As I survey my small garden, lightly dusted with snow, I'm aware of how fragile it has become. Everything is etched sharply in the scene before me. Plants that looked tough and strong are bent slightly in the wind, the spirit gone out of them. Those that stay green, or gray, or burgundy all winter put on a brave show — a symbol of the life continuing below.

This early snow is a mere taste of what's to come. Finally I go inside, to curl up, and start the long winter of reading piles of books and magazines stacked up around the bed. Even when there is little to be done outside, there are pleasures connected with the garden no matter what the season.

Garden fantasy

One of my fantasies is to start a garden *tabula rasa*. If I have fifteen years left to live, there's enough time: it takes five years for a garden to settle down and look established and another ten to mature. I speculate about how I would make it perfect this time.

This time there'd be an area for grandchildren: a tree house, a secret garden, a place of their own. I'd have tall grass for my cat to wander in so she can pretend she's a hunter once again.

I'd certainly have a wild area with nothing but native trees, flowers, and ground covers. A hedgerow of shrubs laden with fruit would form a habitat for all the animals and birds I want to spend my dotage observing.

But I'd also have a garden room for the special plants, the exotics, I dearly love. How could I live without most of the artemisias? Or the Japanese maple? Or the roses?

I'd want a real pond with frogs and fish. A perfect place for insects to find respite. And the sound of water rushing over rocks, subtle and soothing. And a lush woodland.

I would also have a romantic gazebo, a rose arbor, warm walls to espalier fruit and lots of resting niches to admire my handiwork for dreaming away hot summer afternoons.

Garden images

A garden can be inclusive or it can be exclusive. A garden that welcomes you in through a door or arbor, that seduces you inward with a bench or pergola, is an inclusive garden. One with high walls, heavy doors, and plants barring the way is exclusive.

Neither is good nor bad. They are just gardens with different purposes. An exclusive garden can be a cossetting place for its owner. And an inclusive garden may not allow enough privacy for the likes of me.

An inclusive garden invites you in immediately. It is open, almost guileless, and has the easiest of all passages to its glories: no fences, perhaps only an agreeable bower.

I have an exclusive garden. A visitor has to open two garden doors to get into it. One is large enough for a medieval castle keep. The other is just a nice looking finish to the deck. Together they fend off the outside world. But once inside it is a place that I hope makes people feel welcomed into this place I love so dearly.

I've seen inclusive gardens that I admire a great deal. One you can see coming down the street from a great distance. The arbor dripping with roses, plants spilling out onto the street that say, "Get on over here and look." I always do.

I remember walking out early one morning and coming across a garden that beckoned to me. The owner was standing on her porch. "Hi," I said without thinking, "I'm a gardener. May I see your garden?" "Of course," she replied, "What would you like in your coffee?"

A garden gives evidence of the spirit of the owner. Perhaps mine says that I want people to enter my life with great difficulty.

Silence

A fresh fall of snow deadens all the harsh noise of the city. It reminds me how little silence there is left. Years ago, skiing alone on a trail through the woods, I stopped to listen to the sounds around me. What I heard was silence. No birds or animals stirred. There were no other people for miles. It was so quiet that I could hear the snow falling lightly around me. I understood at that moment what it meant to be awestruck. I can't remember having that experience before, certainly not since.

Occasionally in the city, I'm taken aback by how seldom we can even get close to quiet, let alone experience silence. When we call for silence, we are usually begging for less noise. There's always the whine of machinery, the boom of distant construction and a slight rumbling of traffic.

But during these days of new snow, there is surprisingly little noise even in the middle of the city. The only sound may be the slight rustling of grasses long since turned dry and brown and even more graceful than at any other time of the year.

The weeping willow, its long slender branches covered with ice, makes a rushing sound in the breeze. I fall in love with its icy beauty. These are the winter days I adore.

Though I may never hear a profound silence again, I'm happy with a muffled pulse that tells me the city around me is so alive.

Winter walls

In midwinter, gardens are at their most exposed, most fragile. There is something so splayed about them, it almost breaks the heart. Evergreens, those mute testaments to survival, give the garden its winter bones. Though I barely notice them at other times of the year, now I'm immensely grateful they are there.

Along with ivy and euonymus, there are cotoneasters trained up against the walls or spilling out of large wooden containers — anything to break up the midwinter dreariness.

Ivy is one of my favorites. It has elegance. And the old saying — "The first year it sleeps, the second year it creeps, the third year it leaps" — is absolutely true. In our rigorous climate that process may take five or six years before it finally vaults all over the place. What's not to love about this plant? It won't kill healthy trees or weaken a solid wall. It provides shelter for birds. It looks gorgeous against a fall of snow. You can whack off anything that looks dead to reveal the most enchanting new growth.

The Virginia creeper, spectacular in autumn, looks like lacy mesh all winter, hanging off the wires, trailing from telephone poles, a fine contrast with the tidy green ivy.

Then there are the cotoneasters with berries on them. The birds haven't been desperate enough for food just yet, so we can enjoy them for a few more weeks.

In the worst of winter I can always enjoy this lull for one moment longer, sitting bundled up on the back deck, glad to be alive.

The magic of light

I n my climate the hours of daylight are few, the number of sunny hours even fewer. We trudge through the gloom day after day all through January and February. But when the sun does shine, it carries a magnificence unlike any other time. Perhaps our gratitude for light makes it so, but I think not.

The ice on the branches of the birch and the willow makes long silvery streaks in the morning sun. The glinting shards glancing off clean snow dazzle the eye. Statuesque plants that have been left uncut were created for such a day as this. Long shadows made by stalks leaning this way and that form elaborate patterns on the snow like Japanese woodblocks.

Ornamental grasses look frazzled at the edges but the steely blue ones have their color and their shape intact. The long slanting light intensifies the blue.

This is the kind of morning to be out checking things in the garden. To throw another bag of leaves on top of the compost to keep it warm. To see if there are blocks of ice at the bottom of any of the shrubs in the low-lying parts of the garden. To check out the evergreens and make sure they've had enough water. To tie leftover branches from Christmas trees on the southern side of the rhododendrons, protecting them from the harsh sunlight that will hit in March.

Light and snow fulfill my idea of what the garden should look like in winter, crammed with shapes and colors that change constantly. This is the kind of day we wait for all winter long, this brief moment of glory.

Evergreens

One marvel of winter are the evergreens shimmering briskly in the hard midwinter sun. They are background for other plants through most of the year, but now is their own moment of distinction.

Some hold the snow gently in thick branches and make fascinating shadows on the ground. Others form voluptuous shapes under the snow. Put together, they create the choreography of the winter garden.

In northern climates we take evergreens for granted. They are everywhere. Yet evergreens live completely different lives from most other plants. All winter long they breath and transpire moisture. No hibernation or dormancy for them.

If they haven't been deeply watered in the fall before the frost hardens the soil, they suck themselves dry. A kind of self-cannibalization. Twigs and branch tips turn brown, bark shrivels up. A premature aging takes place. Even death.

The pale watery winter sun which seems puny can burn a fragile broad-leaf evergreen if it's unprotected. The warmth of the sun stirs plant cells into action. When temperatures plummet at sunset, the cold expands the moisture in the cells, making them explode. The damage sets in.

Every plant has a survival strategy of its own. It is terribly important to find it out before letting it go unprotected into winter. It's a rare garden where plants, even the ancient ones, don't need some kind of help from us.

The garden and aging

I don't know anyone who's excited about growing old. The wrinkles, the stiff joints, the increasing maladies. But age falls away in the garden.

The body responds to being around plants almost immediately. You feel better. Maybe it's all that oxygen affecting the way the skin feels. It becomes all tingly like the feeling you have coming out of a particularly good sleep when your body comes alive deliciously.

I don't feel any age when I'm in the garden, neither young nor old. I am my most truly vibrant self there. Maybe this is why gardening is so therapeutic for old people or people with disabilities. A garden can accommodate almost anything.

If you are old and crippled, you can always garden in a chair or by raised beds. If you are depressed, a garden will always take you out of a mood. It may not change forever but it will be lifted for a while. Sometimes that's good enough.

If you have no energy, going into a garden can revivify sagging spirits. You start to work without thinking deeply, and before you know it you are getting something done. The garden gives back that vigor and keeps you going.

Now if we can get all of that from a tiny plot of land no bigger than the normal living room, think what a huge park, a forest, or a wilderness can do for the population. Think about what we do to the natural world. We need to open up our imaginations to the infinite possibilities that nature offers us.

The birch in snow

We had a huge snowstorm during the night. The howling winds finally abated and morning broke with a deathly calm. I almost hated to view the damage.

But when I looked out at the garden buried deep beneath the snow, I was enchanted. Hoarfrost hung on every branch. I stared raptly until it became apparent something was seriously wrong. I wasn't sure what for several minutes. The birch tree — it was missing. Had it blown down during the night? A tree can't just disappear.

Bundling up, I slogged with great difficulty to the back of the garden where the birch had stood erect the day before. There it was, lying on its side, bent over with snow, now rapidly turning to ice in the pale sun struggling to shine.

My neighbor came out when she saw me flapping about in panic. "Hang on," she cried, "I'll get our skis." Brilliant. We banged away at the snow and ice for an hour, and slowly the tree managed to come to shoulder height. Slowly, much too slowly, it became more upright with each strike at a branch.

Another hour and we had shaken it loose of ice, back to its position of honor. I was elated that my good old birch survived, standing a little wobbly in place, where it will no doubt remain long after I'm dead.

Garden history

No garden is really new. What we garden on is as ancient as the earth itself. So when we put in a new garden, it's really just rearranging something very old.

Our area is one of dense clay and alluvial silt. It was once at the bottom of a vast lake and as the ice age slowly retreated, glaciers scoured out the bottomland, grinding rocks into shale. Lakes and rivers formed from the runoff. Eons later farms and villages perched on the edge. But as the city grew around them, they were filled in and covered over. This glorious past has been almost obliterated.

The urge to rid ourselves of history is puzzling. We've covered and cemented and rerouted rivers and streams, bending them to our own will. The old practise of building with the contours of the land was forgotten when our city was designed by army engineers in the eighteenth century. Those fellows believed in grids. So we have grids that ignore the land forms.

I think about this when the garden emerges in late winter. This ancient place must have been haunting when it was a pond filled with birds. Then, in the nineteenth century, it became a fruit farm. If you stand on the roof of the house, you can still see the pattern of the fruit trees as they burst into bloom in the spring.

The other day one of these trees, at least a hundred years old, certainly a hundred feet tall, was cut down. This huge tree committed the crime of throwing shade on a swimming pool. It was dirty as well — constantly dropping leaves into the water. And so went another small but significant connection with our past.

Winter solstice

I cannot shake off the mood of deep despair I fall into as the winter solstice approaches. I understand with the bottom of my heart why people had to light candles against the forces of chaos that seem to be all around. It gets darker and darker earlier each day.

There is a closing in on oneself as though swaddled up in your own blackness will save you from falling off the edge. Christmas is coming and is the only distraction from these long gloom-ridden nights.

It's easy to understand why our primitive ancestors picked this time of year for the most lavish, glittering festival their lively imaginations could come up with. We struggle now as to whether it's better to have a real tree or a plastic one.

I'd rather identify with the ancients in this case and feel the threatening darkness all around me. I don't want to see family or friends, or talk to neighbors. It's too much effort. I certainly don't want to wander in the brightly lit stores swamped with forced bonhomie and tinny Christmas music. I want to be encapsulated by my own house with the heat turned up too high, eating chocolate.

And so I stay at home for days on end waiting for the solstice to pass. Waiting so I can cheerfully announce, "Well, the days are getting shorter and spring will be here soon." And I turn the lights on in the garden and watch them hold back the darkness for a few hours longer.

Cardinals

The tag end of winter leaves the garden as gray, brown, and tattered as I feel. Nothing looks particularly good. Bits of dirty snow, the limp stalks left over from the fall — everything looks messy.

Suddenly a pair of cardinals, brilliant in scarlet, illuminate the whole garden. Transfixed, I stand and watch for twenty minutes as they dart from one failed plant to another, winkling out precious seeds. They flash from branch to branch of the *Rosa glauca*. This had been their own territory earlier in the winter. No other birds dared touch the huge orange hips. The cardinals have doled them out one or two at a time, eking out a living from the garden.

I was sure there was nothing more for them here, but they've found something. One stays on the fence, while the other forages. Then they switch places.

On our dark days these flashes of scarlet seem almost *outré*. Why does this bird have such plumage when everything else looks so dull? It makes me stop and take a new look at everything outside.

My numbed eye had failed to see that the whole place is still filled with riches. I stopped berating the garden for my own sour mood. The tall grasses looked almost pink in the pale sunlight. The mahonia was turning from its winter burgundy to a darker shade and would soon turn brown again. But that doesn't bother me now that I've been buoyed by the sight of these extravagant birds.

Formal gardens

I visit the same garden every year when we are in France. It's a very large, very formal garden. Designed to impress. And each year, sitting in this opulent surround, I find myself grateful that I don't have all these clipped hedges, stiff topiary, and trained vines in my own garden. It speaks of a tidy, highly *organized* mind.

My garden doesn't look organized and that's the intention. I want it to look spontaneous, completely different with each season. What a contrast to this one. Here, every season looks pretty much the same to my eye. The enclosure of the parterres are relaxing but they are meant to show off people, not plants. Each view is fully enveloped with a circle, square, or opening of greenery to pull your eye towards it.

The hand behind this garden has such a vise-like grip that there seems little space for experimenting and, worst of all, no room for making mistakes. In this tortured environment anything out of place or slightly loopy would look terrible.

I do draw the line here though about knot gardens — low hedges planted in fanciful patterns. They are often the major element in a formal garden and are really quite humane and sensual. They can be applied to most gardens in a lot of different materials.

I look at my front garden and fancy a little knot garden out there just to change the scene. It's exactly the crazy kind of symbiosis I like. An untidy old silver maple and a pristine little knot garden. But that's as far as I'm willing to go. I don't think I could live full-time with a formal garden no matter how hard I tried.

Death

When I die, I want to be cremated and have my ashes scattered around the garden for slug bait. I'd like a little sign saying: As useful in death as she was in life. This isn't funny to my kids.

But somehow when you're in the garden all the time, you get used to thinking about death. You're usually busy bumping off some creature or another, willingly or not.

Thinking about death doesn't depress me. It's just there. I don't want my garden to die, but of course it will. I asked a great gardener, now in her eighties, what she'd do with her garden, and she replied breezily, "It will die with me." *No*, I wanted to shout — but of course it will. And, she pointed out, Sissinghurst is not Vita Sackville-West's garden anymore, it's the garden of those who garden there.

I'd like to think that whoever took over this garden would like what I've done enough to keep at least a ghost of me in the form I've imposed on the space. But as a gardener I'd be pretty interested to see what someone else could do with it as well. There's one gardener I know who left her plants to a wise friend with instructions that he distribute them to other gardeners who would appreciate them as once having been a part of her.

I rather like the idea. But we aren't used to bequeathing plants. Yet I can see the day coming. I like to let my mind wander over who might like the bits and pieces of this garden. It's not my immortality. A garden is too ephemeral for that. But being slug bait, now *that's* ambitious.

A seminal book

Most people have one book of which they can say, "This is the one that changed my life." For me, that book is *The Education of a Gardener* by Russell Page, published in 1962. I found it in a second hand store a few years later and thought it was an interesting but odd idea — to write about a life in gardening.

At that time, I was only marginally interested in the garden; it had always been essentially the children's playground. But Page's writing entranced me. His clarity of thought and tone, his unpretentiousness, made engrossing reading. It became a book that I reread the way one does Jane Austen — every few years — because it's good for the soul and sets you right about many things other than its purported subject.

Page's ideas about garden design opened up the possibility that I might make a garden too. I had no idea who he was or that he was one of the most significant garden designers of the century. I absorbed his taste and style without even knowing it was happening. Was I a Russellite? A Pagist?

When this decision hit — to have something more than the strip of grass with flower borders along each side that had been with us for seventeen years — it seemed daunting. What few gardens I had seen were historical, important beyond anything possible.

Page's message was to trust one's aesthetic, to apply it to the space around and make it anew. And, best of all, to live a life surrounded by enormous vitality and color, something that I could make myself, by myself. I turned my thoughts to the garden and started imagining the possibilities.

Christmas in the garden

Christmas is an especially poignant time of the year in the garden. It will look beautiful to my eye whether it's a green or a white Christmas. The brilliant scarlet berries on the cotoneaster, the rich orange fruits of firethorn and bittersweet, look like faux jewelry amidst all the brown vines and the white of new fallen snow.

I know that in a few weeks birds desperate for food will sweep through and, in one day, consume the last of this treasure. It's important to keep on reminding myself that the garden isn't closed down, that life is flourishing underneath the matted leaves and fallen stalks.

The compost looks frozen solid from the outside, but when I shove my hand deep into the center I can feel its heat and know that there is life still thriving there.

I gather up bits of vine to make a wreath and attach whatever is left in the garden to it — a tangle of artemisia, a dried-up bit of dead blossom denuded of its seeds. I figure out just how much I'll decorate indoors to satisfy my own sense of the season. Then calculate how quickly I can get the ropes of cedar, the spruce boughs, the old wreaths that are falling apart back into the garden. Nature recycling nature.

The feeling of decay is everywhere yet somehow it smacks of new life. I can feel the breath of spring, if ever so faint, and all its possibilities thrill me far more than the season of joy.

A garden epiphany

An epiphany is considered one of the most important of all religious experiences. A religious epiphany is when everything comes together almost in a blinding insight and you know something to be true. I believe I've had one attached to a garden experience. A garden epiphany is in that league. It's *knowing* what you want of a garden — in an instant — and knowing this is right and true for you and your land. It's the seeing of something entirely, something that wasn't there before.

My epiphany came in the dead of winter while staring out at the backyard. I suddenly saw the garden: divided into rooms, a checkerboard pattern in place, an intense planting of trees, shrubs and perennials making a living picture — in vivid color. Since I had never seriously gardened before, I was shocked by what I saw.

How could I, a neophyte, possibly create something like this picture as it appeared in my mind's eye? I looked at the paintings in my house and though I can't paint, I can appreciate paintings. I've learned a lot from looking at paintings. I thought that maybe if I learned about gardening, I could make a garden painting.

That was in 1986. I had only a few garden books, so I bought more. I loved the pictures. I had never seen gardens like that, certainly not in the city where I live.

The more ardently I gardened, the more I met other gardeners who astonished me with their knowledge and wisdom. I found a network of people with a passion unlike anything I'd come across before. I made new friends, I changed my life — because of an epiphany on a cold winter morning.

The beauty of Latin names

I love to hear the sound of Latin names rolling off a gardener's tongue. I don't have much patience for the snobs who speak only in Latin, or for the reverse snobs who won't use anything but common names. Neither camp is much fun.

But when you hear someone calmly pointing out a plant and giving its full name, so it's not just gobbledygook, that's pure pleasure. At first, I didn't understand the fuss about using full botanical names. Just one of those eccentric things about old-time gardeners. But it's now evident that to know the correct name (even if you don't use it all the time) is very important.

It's not immediately easy to understand botanical Latin. But think of where the names come from. In early Roman times Pliny and his crowd were giving plants names to describe the country of origin and location, therefore what kind of needs they would have.

It's neither snobby nor meant to be intimidating to know a bit of Latin. It is, however, hell pronouncing it properly. Because there's one thing a gardener can be counted on for — to correct all pronunciation. The first time I said cotoneaster out loud, I said, "Cotton Easter." Wrongo. It's *co-tone-e-aster*. Now anything else sounds strange. It takes training to have the ear of a gardener but you learn a lot when you do. And you can travel anywhere in the world with botanical Latin and be understood.

Catalogues

Years ago, as a guest on a TV show, I referred to many of the garden catalogues I was displaying as "garden porn." I'd used the term before in a book review and no one objected. But the people on this show cut out the offending term.

Catalogues are so glossy, so luscious, so colorful and glamorous that they suck you in, push you further on the road to temptation. Like porn but not so harmful.

Plants don't look as good as they do in catalogues for a couple of years. Maybe more. You probably aren't going to be able to grow half this stuff because you're living in the wrong place anyway. What actually arrives by mail looks half dead. Nothing magnificent about this.

Too discouraging, you might think. But no. The catalogues come in and ritualistically I gather them all up around my bed and go through them with yellow stickers marking everything I like — double flagging those I have a definite letch for.

I fool myself with this busyness — sort of — I'm making price comparisons. But what I'm really on the prowl for is something unusual, something I can't get at my favorite nursery, and hope, usually foolishly, that I'll be the first in my crowd to possess it.

I cannot do without catalogues. They are crucial to long winter nights. And I'll continue to order way too much. I'm not quite sure where I'm going to put everything. For gardeners, being led into temptation is not necessarily the best way to go but it's a lot of fun.

Weeds

One country's weeds are another's garden escapees. This never fails to amuse me when I'm in the south of France. We walk up a steep hill to our favorite restaurant, a truck stop with the best view of the Riviera and prices we can afford.

To get to our café, we go past the *marché,* the cemetery, and up steep steps to the *moyenne corniche.* Along the way are wildings that I look after very carefully in my own garden: angelica that grows to huge proportions, the dreaded acanthus, and the lovely but invasive oxalis, poppies, nasturtiums, and a mallow that looks like a monster.

There is a euphorbia that has escaped the garden and naturalized itself all over the hills in the area. Its yellow blends perfectly with the broom that sweeps across the terraces and hillsides next to the olive trees.

All these things are well behaved in the garden at home, but here they are seen as pests, something to root out and get rid of. Some plants simply aren't valued until they've been put into a garden and shown off to their best advantage. And others will stay as weeds no matter where you put them.

The controlling hand

The controlling hand, to me, is meant in an ironic way. Normally the controlling hand is any touch made by people. We make deliberate changes to control what is around us. The minute we set about to make a garden we inevitably disturb the natural order of things. We can't use machines to scour off the tops of hills and not expect violent change. We can't cut down trees along lakes, rivers and streams and not expect to witness terrifying erosion.

I don't mean these great disturbances, however, when I think of the controlling hand. I think about working within a system. A very gentle touch.

The controlling hand, as I see it, makes a big effort to keep out of things. To hold back, to wait, to observe what's happening within the system even in a small backyard. Maybe even more important for a small space. Because there the controlling hand really does have almost complete control.

This planet is an exquisitely arranged and interconnected system. What's controlled in one place is going to have consequences in another place. Our job as gardeners is to try and figure this out no matter how small our allotted space might be.

Discipline has to be the watchword for our controlling hands. It means not gardening without thinking of the garden as habitat: for mice, for squirrels, for bees and wasps. For other living creatures beyond ourselves.

To have a controlling hand in future gardens will mean more patient observance, more time spent in contemplation of what the site is offering than high voltage energy and instant results.

Plants in paintings

A s a twenty-one-year-old, I bought a painting that's influenced the way I look at nature more than anything else. This painting by Louis de Niverville has a scene by the sea filled with exotic plants. Most of them fantasies dreamed up by the artist.

There is a red-checkered tablecloth in the middle of the painting and there are two women solemnly looking out from the center. The older I get the more I look like them. At first this painting led me to fill my house with plants. And I started looking at other paintings with great bouquets of flowers in them: more artists' fantasies — these flowers couldn't possibly all bloom together so conveniently. But I liked the idea of making garden pictures. Something dreamed up by Gertrude Jekyll, a complete stranger to me at the time.

As I slowly made the transition from house plants to having all my plants out of doors, I got involved with designing the garden. When I made my first real composition with plants, the central image was a checkerboard. I don't know if I got the idea subliminally from this painting, or if I saw it in a book. Not that either matters. More important, this indicates to me just how much looking at works of art can influence a gardener's taste.

I did know through years of working in a gallery that the more you look at works of art, the keener your eye becomes. The more of a sense of composition you will develop and a better sense of color will eventually force its way into your being.

When I started to garden I kept all of these firmly in my mind. Sometimes, on a really good day, I think I might get there.

Sunsets

What I lack at home I find during the winter in France: the vista, the sea, the sunsets that go on seemingly for hours. I am mesmerized by cloud formations and just what moment they will deepen and become infused by the last rays of the sun as it sinks behind the hills beyond the bay in front of me. How fantastically the light changes the little houses on the surrounding hillside.

Sunsets mean different things when you're in different places. I think of all the other sunsets I've seen. Of being in Arizona in a city of concrete with no green, no place to stop and stare at the daily magnificence that lasts for hours over the desert. Surely a place constructed by people who never saw the beauty of the place, only its development potential.

Or the sunsets of Labrador where the horizon was so vast and the panoply of color so varied that only the aurora borealis could compete in its palette.

At home, a sunset is such a bonus I think about it for days. Most times I feel bereft because I have only the reflected sunset bouncing off the trees, and I feel cut off from a certain reality.

Sunsets in other people's homes or places are the beginning of the evening, or the end of the day, drawing on what's been most pleasurable in the past. We attach a great many emotions to sunsets, I've found.

Life without sunsets would be grim. People go on about the sunset years of life; I hope mine will be blazing with light and color.

Acanthus

The huge fleshy leaves of the acanthus are much revered in all cultures around the Mediterranean. The leaves are etched into friezes, molded to columns, and melded into pottery. It has been the symbol of regeneration from pre-Roman times to the present.

Dating back from our first visit to the south of France I have tried to grow *Acanthus mollis* in my own garden. I want to have a little bit of that feeling of an area I find so gorgeous. But it's tough going in a shady garden.

I do my acanthus adoration on the hillsides around the place we stay each year. Or I did until I visited my friend William. He has a garden close to the Italian border. On one of my annual visits he and a friend were hacking out large stands of acanthus. "This is our very worst weed," he said. "It will fracture concrete." As indeed it had with his driveway. Huge rifts had appeared in what looked like fairly new tarmac.

The roots of the acanthus as they were exposed were enormous, tough, almost evil-looking things. This opened my formerly rose-glazed eyes. I suddenly saw them everywhere: the railway tracks, down the sides of neglected slopes, popping through crumbling walls, splitting ancient palm trees apart. Almost anyplace there wasn't a gardener keeping it at bay.

How could anything so sensual, so innocuous looking, be so lethal? Near us the acanthus is hacked down summarily just before it might bloom. The plants come back within a week or so, a further testament to their resilience.

When something is taken out of context it can seem very harmless, like an acanthus in my own garden. But when you see it where it can live unchecked you realize what a menace even a plant can be.

Picking wildflowers

There are wonderful walks around the seawalls of the cape where we visit in France. The wild waves crash directly below and the cliffs above soar to the villas of the very, very rich. But you feel safe because the walkways are so well designed.

Not safe though are the wildflowers that grow in every opening, typical of the south of France. The soil is chockablock with so many nutrients it will support almost anything.

It's the Sunday walkers who are dangerous. They pick the lady slippers in March with no thought to the future of these plants.

I want to say: "No, no. If you pick them, you kill the entire plant and they will never return." But how to say it judiciously, without giving offense when I'm a guest in this country. Words always seem to fail on these occasions.

I have absolutely no hesitation at home to caution people who steal seeds from public parks. I've watched this go on right in front of a park director's eyes. Some people have no shame. It doesn't occur to them to ask, to find out if these seeds are going to be harvested for a special purpose.

The attitude in both cases is that this is public, therefore you own the right to pick anything that grows or to collect the seeds anywhere you find them.

But the very worst offense it seems are those people who go into the woods or other wild places and dig up whole stands of plants to sell, or maybe just to keep or even share. There is a rule of thumb among gardeners that if an area is to be destroyed, by every means possible get the plants out of there and into good homes. But let them alone and don't buy plants that have been collected in the wild.

Antecedents

No gardener springs from whole cloth. We have antecedents no matter how tenuous they may be. I find more and more gardeners who tell me that no one in their family ever gardened. They have no idea where this passion came from.

I would have said the same thing a few years ago. But when I look back on my family history, I find my family always gardened — after a fashion. My grandfather kept bantam show-cockerels in his Vancouver backyard, much to the distress of his neighbors who put up with sunrise serenades for decades. The day after he died, my grandmother rung the necks of four of the noisiest ones. At eighty-nine, she set out to install flower beds where chicken coops once stood and generally improve and enlarge her garden.

From her I learned that you don't throw anything away, you put it in a pile and then you can put it back in the garden. We didn't know it was called composting at the time, but the lesson stuck.

During World War II, all of us kids were encouraged to have Victory gardens. I think it was to grow our own food. Or maybe it was to make us feel we were part of the war effort, along with saving all the string and silver paper we could (a habit I can't break to this day).

My parents always had a vegetable garden but I don't remember any flowers or even huge harvests of vegetables. It was one of those money-saving burdens, not a balm to war-torn souls. It was a duty. No wonder I didn't grow up with an instinctive love of gardening. It's not in the genes. You've got to love it to do it properly.

Pleasure of the eye

I'm a great believer in understanding some of the principles of design when it comes to making a garden. If you have a sense of composition, you probably can't go wrong. This includes a feeling for scale, how things relate to one another, and the uses of positive and negative space.

All well and good, but then there's the pleasure of the eye. Somehow you just seem to know when two plants will look ravishing together. You are never quite sure where that knowledge comes from. Stolen? Experiment? It doesn't matter.

The longer you garden the better that eye gets, the more tuned to how colors vibrate in different ways and what they can do to each other. You become a scientist as well as an artist, with the lines between increasingly blurred.

Gardeners never feel they've "finished" a garden. That's not in the lexicon. They feel they might have done as much as can be done for now, knowing that later on whole areas of the garden will have to be ripped up and started over again. Taste shifts, things will look askew. A favorite color will fade and something else becomes more compelling. Time to start again.

It's not important to study gardens to make one, though that helps. It's important to explore this pleasure of the eye, developing a feel for plants. Then, and this is most important, the actual doing of it.

Winter bouquets

I'm not very creative when it comes to making up bouquets. My standards aren't very high — anything shoved into a bowl or vase looks pretty good to me.

But when it comes to forcing plants during the long winter months, I become ambitious. I like prowling about in the garden in winter looking for anything that might come into bloom or leaf out earlier than if it's left outside.

Going to the farmers' market or driving into the country becomes a challenge to find something to gussy up the drabness of the house. Pussy willows come to mind. Forsythia is the traditional plant to cut in our area. Wild roses will form leaves, as will dogwood, witch hazel, and corkscrew hazel with its fascinating shape. Since I have the giant weeping willow I like to use great long fallen fronds as background shapes and add an elegant note.

And you don't have to do violence to most branches, like smashing them up as is the custom (it just makes more room for bacteria to develop). A clean cut and clear filtered water are all that's needed.

What's fascinating is the genetic code that responds to the slightest rise in temperature to start a whole new cycle right before your eyes. Somehow it's easier to really look at leaves unfurling when you have a vase on the table in front of you for several days. You can see almost microscopic buds stretching out, elongating, searching for the sun.

When this happens I know that winter will be over soon and I can go back to being tranquil with the knowledge that the whole garden is my bouquet.

Winter finales

I like to stare at the winter garden, to imagine what lives continue as yet another storm rages about. I think of the mice that must be running somewhere about. I can see the little tunnels beneath the snow. Do they stay in the compost where it's warm?

As the snow melts, winter damage is painfully obvious: bark splits, plants are humped right out of the ground by freeze-thaw cycles. This does more harm than even the most ferocious storms. The plant starts to be released from the frozen earth where it's been sleeping. Then suddenly the warming stops and the freezing begins again. The moisture in the earth expands and forces the soil upward — along with the plant.

Winterkill is one of those dramatic horticultural terms that make you think of corpses strewn about a battlefield. This is, for once, an overstatement. All it means is that the plant wasn't hardened off early enough before the onslaught. Then tips, twigs, even branches can die off. But it's not the end of the world, let alone the plant.

I look, as well, for any signs that describe the end of winter. From my kitchen window, when I see a heath I know I'll survive. The sighting of this glorious slash of color against the last snow signals winter's end. Given winter ravages, the gardener must play a waiting game to see what's going to stir into life and what will simply have to be eliminated. It also means spring promise.

We have this sense that winter goes on forever. It doesn't, it just feels that way. The erica is a signal to mush through the snow to cut branches for forcing and a whole new season starts to come forward indoors. Without these gifts of life, the last few months would be intolerable.

Spring

Rebirth

hrough the inevitable crises that life presents, I've always thought of myself as emerging as though reborn. Here I am whole again, renewed, bloodied but not bowed. If I'd had a garden earlier in life, how much easier things would have been.

Gardeners face the concept of rebirth every year. It awakens all their senses to the possibility of renewal, and that, this time, they'll get it right.

It's a lovely idea that you constantly get second chances in gardening. You always look forward to the next season. You think about change for its own sake and change to make whatever you touch more graceful, more dazzling.

The idea of rebirth exists in every culture and every religion. It helps to have this concept firmly entrenched in the way we live — how else would we be able to carry on?

Gardening has long been an obvious metaphor for this rebirth. In medieval times gardening, as we know it, was invented. Nuns and monks used gardening as part of their sense of worship. And that has persisted among the gardeners I know.

Whether they belong to an organized religion or not, they are always intensely spiritual people. As though to garden is to understand and worship nature or the forces that are beyond our own control. It is to acknowledge that we are a part of this huge mysterious miracle of annual renewal.

And when each crisis hits I look into the garden and see that it's not the end of the world yet, just a changing of seasons.

Early spring

In the early morning, just as the sun is rising, as it filters through the trees in long shafts, I am once again consumed by rapture at this, the best time of the day.

In the garden I can see things of such strange beauty I am filled with awe. The fragile tips of the very first hostas push their way through the cold, damp soil. The contortions of leaves as they twist themselves away from the earth are like exquisite silk — opaque and luminous. With the pale morning sun behind them, it makes my heart almost burst with the pure joy of a new day and a new season. Though I honor hostas for their statuesque beauty, they never again have quite the same delicate quality.

All through the woodland there is the stream of narcissus — the satiny yellows and white — to accompany the intense cobalt blue velvet of the muscari. This is my small bit of embroidery.

I crawl about on the face of the earth, moving old leaves out of the way searching for all the signs of new life. Everywhere there are tiny things pushing upwards, so small and delicate I wonder how they'll ever survive.

I look for weeds, but it's unbearable to remove anything. Surely everything is important right now. I leave things alone and just tidy up by stroking the soil with an old pair of leather gloves so nothing gets disturbed too much. This is just the parting of the ways to allow the sun to warm things up.

I reflect on the sense of burgeoning. And I feel so completely alive. Always, the gardener is the lucky one to have this sense of another new beginning.

Spring cleanup

The first sweet smell of the earth warming up sweeps over the garden. There is no other smell like this one. I'm restless, filled with spring fever, glad to be out of the house and into the sun.

I dart about, doing this and then that. I know I should be working on one small space at a time. But the garden is spread out before me with every square inch demanding something.

Here's a vine winding its way through a shrub. It looked wonderful all winter long, like a gloriously tatty stole. Now it merely looks dead and needs to be cut right back to the ground.

There are also vines that must be pruned at once so they will have blossoms later on. Anything blooming on new wood won't produce a thing worth thinking about if they aren't whacked away at immediately. Other vines must be left alone. Every year I forget which is which. Maybe cute little tags with "Cut Me in Spring" would help. I never seem to get around to it. The winter mulch needs to be removed and thrown back into the compost bin. Something to be done later.

Then there are the fabulous plans I made during the winter: new things to install; which section to redevelop completely; what plants should be divided and where to put them. Great on paper, but slightly more daunting now that I can get outside and see exactly how bad things are.

I can exhaust myself with random energy. Pick up something, put it down somewhere else. But it's all part of spring fever. I'll settle down in a few days and actually get to work. Meanwhile I love this dreamy pointless phase of the gardening year.

Defining spring

Everyone has a personal definition of what spring is and just when it happens. For some, it's the first snowdrop lifting its head above the snow. But that's too early for me. It's rushing the season. I like to linger at the end of winter in a spirit of anticipation at what's to come.

One side of the garden is warmer than the other, so I spend my time in the sun slowly moving dead leaves and other winter accumulation aside to see what's coming up. Nothing can be handled quickly or with a heavy hand because these first small appearances of bulbs are the most precious.

This is a time to contemplate what's been going on under the soil all these long months now the delicate root hairs have been released from ice and frozen soil. I imagine them welcoming the warmth of sun as much as I do. And then pushing their way towards it to get the good of all those rays.

Even though the garden looks disreputable, I go at it one small space at a time — cutting off the stalks that have been let go all winter, checking out what insects have been living there and hoping it's something benevolent when a sleepy bug comes crawling out.

It's all promise right now. The promise that maybe there won't be the one last snowstorm that takes us by surprise every year. That the rains will hold off until the ground thaws and can absorb the water. That the squirrels will have left some of the hundreds of bulbs planted last fall. It's all spring and all spilling over with life and it fills me with ecstasy.

Spring bulbs

Spring smells of earth. Of dampness. Of brown. A smell with slight overtone of decay. A hint of mist rises from the soil as the newly warmed air touches the still-cool ground. I find the first signs of bulbs coming up — their delicate tips a rich green against the sombre backdrop of soil.

I'm always amazed when they do come up. The idea that a bulb comes to us with everything needed for survival is one of those minor miracles. You need to do nothing. All the genetic material to make them what they are, all the food they'll require for that first year, even the shape of the future flower itself is curled up inside that fleshy object you can hold in one hand.

The idea that there is also enough power in that little bulb to shove a fairly stiff stem through soil that's had snow and ice leaning against it all winter is yet another miracle. When I see those first tips I know we're safe, that spring really will come and we'll live through another glorious season.

As bulbs struggle their way through the soil, the beady little eyes of my squirrels are watching. As the first new blooms of tulips just make it, opening up, they strike. I wake to a dawn of broken tulip heads. I swear they prefer red to all other colors.

The narcissus are poison to them, and they leave most things planted nearby alone so I don't feel as responsible to those bulbs as I do the poor tulips. Keeping this rugged life in mind makes anything I go through during the day look easy by comparison.

Revenge of nature

Nature will get its own back. People say something of that sort when a tree trunk breaks through a wall or falls on a car, or a monsoon floods out hapless peasants in some faraway country. That we've chosen to build in the path of a tough root system, or that people have always lived in the paths of monsoons, isn't taken into account. It's breathtaking how nature is looked upon as an adversary and not something we are part of.

When our old neighbor was alive she had three lots behind us filled with trees, shrubs, and every imaginable wild and woodland plant. We had no idea that she had also created a complex ecosystem capable of absorbing heavy spring rains. And, it turned out, was crucial to keeping the flood plain we live on in check. Or that the trees she grew in such profusion were a habitat for many animals, including bugs and birds.

When she died her heirs promptly turned this glorious tangle into a parking lot and sold off the houses. And so the annual floods began. The children loved it. Bridges were built, boats were floated during these flood days. As I became a more sophisticated gardener I noted our lots are a flypast for dozens of species of birds swooping in to take advantage of a drink and food on their way north.

Somehow working with that disaster helped create an attitude in all our family that nature is a friend to be made, not an enemy. The flood, in its way, was also an act of revenge, something brought on by people just like ourselves. It's painful to know that we've done this everywhere so thoughtlessly.

The spring mess

Sometimes it can be discouraging to be a gardener. One minute you have a garden bursting with the dazzling blossoms of narcissus, tulips, muscari, scilla — all the little bulbs. The next minute the same blooms look decidedly brown around the edges propped up by dun-colored foliage that threatens to linger for months.

The foliage stays with us to store up the needed food for the survival of next year's flowers. The minute the offending disarray is lopped off, the plant is doomed. They must be left alone.

I've seen lots of attempts at making this clutter look well behaved. Braiding foliage is one. A completely braided garden is impressive, almost cheeky in its assumption. But the amount of work required for this is way beyond me.

Wrapping them up with rubber bands is another. But it strikes me that the rubber band would cut off the circulation in the plant's vascular system. And even if it doesn't, it looks mean. Tying them into little knots is too fussy by far and accomplishes the same pinched look.

So I'm stuck with this spring mess. I plant bulbs next to almost anything that will start growing early and hide the shame: roses to distract the eye; lambs' ears with the soft velvety fur; hostas to poke their way aggressively through almost any barrier. Eventually, I give up and head for the last resort — masses of white impatiens to give the whole garden a lift. I don't want to disturb the rhythms of nature but sometimes aesthetics get in the way of being a natural gardener. I want beauty and I want it now.

Dawn

There are days when I walk into the garden and feel ravished by its beauty. Each garden has its own moment of perfection and my garden is most brilliant at first light. It begins as the sun moves over the trees, reaching into surrounding trees and shrubs.

No one else has seen the garden in this moment of perfection. It's become an intimate moment for me. The sun, diffused among the plants, seems to light them from within. The whole place is bathed in a luminosity so complete it makes me catch my breath.

I could never become too familiar, never take this sacred moment for granted. There are times when I wake in the dead of night and yearn for the moment when I can get up and walk out into the quiet morning air.

The throb of the city is at its gentlest at this time of day. The whine of engines and machinery is hours away. I feel suspended, alone in the midst of this vast city. Narcissistically, I feel that there is no one up but me.

This is when I become my best self. I can do anything with this day and feel fresh, almost pure in the morning's warmth.

Evening ritual

We love to eat in the garden every warm evening until it's too cold in fall. We confine ourselves to a few simple rituals. First we have a glass of wine, and then Jack says to me, "Your eyes are darting about, stop moving plants around." We change places and I pay attention to him.

This sharing of the day by sitting in the garden is something that has become so important to me I resent it when we get rained indoors. The barbecue is in the alley and I throw stuff on it — nothing fancy. We eat wonderful simple meals surrounded by madly sensual scent and color.

Then it's our habit to take a walk around the garden as the light is fading. Jack is not a gardener. His office has the best view of the garden. And occasionally he says, "It's looking good." In all the years of my gardening, he's never learned the name of one plant. But then I don't need him for praise of the garden. He's a writer; I need him to read what I write.

He doesn't interfere with my gardening, he just nods and smiles. I don't know how people cope with two garden egos in any one family. I couldn't stand the interference.

When we walk arm in arm through the garden I show him what I've moved around, where I might put something new, and try not to get carried away going on endlessly about some new plan, or a new and unusual plant. Is he listening? I don't care. It's the taking pleasure in each other's company that counts.

Answers

At some time during my life I've known all the answers to the obvious questions. What makes the sky blue? Why is grass green? How are waves made? What makes a flower red, or yellow, or blue? I knew when I knew the answers that I should be a grandmother right then and there, but it was too early.

And now I'm having to learn the answers all over again. I simply put them somewhere out of sight when my own children were finished with nonstop questioning.

But how do you answer a child's question about such important things without being pedantic? Or if you feel vague about your information, dismissive? You can't just hand them a book. Though books help.

Taking a little kid on a walk brings out all of these questions and more. What makes berries red? Why do roses have thorns? Why do plants climb up walls? Where do birds go at night?

I remember being told sharply, "Don't ask so many questions." And I knew the answer to that was, "How'm I supposed to learn everything if I don't." But I fell silent — and then sought out adults who would tell me things. I felt they were sharing something really important with me — their information, their knowledge. It made me feel terribly privileged.

My kids say I told them too much, made it too hard, spoiled the fun. So I'm relearning the learning. I'm getting ready for the next generation's questions. This time I hope I have enough information to get it right and make it all a lot of fun — for them as well as for me.

Cutting down a tree

We cut down the old maple tree and I spent the day in mourning. It was starting to rot from within and it had to go. I saved this tree from certain death thirty years ago. It was a hacked-up miserable stump of a thing with three spindly sprouts growing from the base.

The placement was good — about a third of the way through the garden — so I decided to do my best to help it. The maple flourished into an imposing creature.

I became a deadly serious gardener and suddenly that tree looked like something that was scooping all the water, the food, and the space I wanted for a lot of other plants. But I was patient, biding my time for twenty years before even entertaining the idea that this tree had to go. I had it carefully pruned. It got everything, plenty of compost, just like anything else in the garden. But in recent years it started showing telltale signs that this second lifetime was coming to an end.

For the ultimate chop, I waited until most of my neighbors were at their cottages. I wanted no criticism about this. It was hard enough to do without that. And I let my nearest neighbor have all the firewood he wanted for free.

Once the huge tree was cleared out I could see what it had been hiding — a scraggly old spruce, a falling down fence. But the whole place looked airier, as though there was more breathing space.

I planted another tree immediately, a good city tree. A gorgeous little ginkgo. It's wise not to get too sentimental over plants and certainly not too attached to them.

Color

I am not crazy about a garden that's a riot of color. The kind where the eye darts about from one great mass of richness to another only to end up spinning in the socket. It may have an impact but it doesn't make me want to spend time in it.

A good garden, like a great painting, will unfold itself with infinite subtlety, never revealing its secrets all at once. Color is essential even in a garden which appears to have little more than, say, green and white.

But nature is much too clever. There are a thousand tones of white, perhaps tens of thousands of green. They shift every minute of the day. What looks like one shade in the morning light, looks completely different in late afternoon. Do you keep this in mind as you put plants in? Perhaps, but I hadn't thought about it until recently.

In the making of my own garden, it happened this way: I started with a need for very strong colors. Bright pinks, magenta, purple, reds, blues. The longer I lived with these colors, the more overwhelming they became. They made me feel raced up at a time of day when I wanted serenity. I moved them further and further away.

I replaced them with softer colors — yellows, white, silvers, gray, and blue. The calming colors for a quiet time in the evening. I found out by experiments, not color charts, what would go best with what. And, from experience, what I need each color for. In gardening, as in everything else, it takes special patience and masses of time to get the right outcome.

Plant obsessions

All gardeners are slightly crazed. They toil in sun and rain for hours on end without noticing. They spend every available cent on a plot of land without giving it a second thought. And they will collect plants.

Plant-obsessed persons are the craziest ones I know. There are some who won't look at a plant if it's over two inches wide. Others will spend a fortune looking for every species in a genus — even if they are ugly. I know gardeners who botanize, or study plants, in the remotest parts of Patagonia if it means seeing a favorite flower in bloom in its natural site.

I also know people who will smuggle plants into the country even though it's illegal. They clip a little leaf there, find seed here, and take a cutting from almost anything. All things they can't find anywhere at home. But the less said of this the better.

Then there's the obsessed gardener who won't do without something rare and unusual. This is the call to be totally and utterly foolish. Like spending a fortune on a plant just to have it first. I plead guilty. It was *Hakonechloa macra* 'Aureola,' a glorious yellow grass that cost thirty-five dollars one year and was six dollars the next. My plant, however, was thriving, ready to be divided, before anyone else could get their hands on it. It's now rather common and I seldom point it out anymore.

Collecting plants is like collecting anything else: you have to keep it under control, or before you know it, collecting takes over your life completely.

The earth's skin

To some, the earth's delicate skin is just dirt, something to be dug up or covered over as quickly as possible. Preferably with concrete. In our backyards no law governs how we treat this frail crust. We can dump chemicals all over it, leave it bare to become eroded, or cover it with all kinds of rusting junk. We can be pig ignorant about it, as we used to say.

Soil is a resource, a living, breathing entity that, if treated properly, will maintain itself. It's our lifeline for survival. When it has finally been depleted, the human population will disappear.

Soil is filled with life: microbes, bacteria, fungi, earthworms, minerals and gases, plus thousands and thousands of other life forms we don't even know about yet. These inhabitants, organic and inorganic, work together in exquisite harmony — if we don't interfere with them.

When we use chemicals to get rid of something we don't like or find distasteful, we risk destroying this balance. Once we mess with one part of the soil, we affect another, and not necessarily for the best.

Project your imagination into the soil below you next time you go into the garden. Think with compassion of the life that exists there. Think, the drama, the sexuality, the harvesting, the work that carries on ceaselessly. Think then about the meaning of being a steward for the earth.

Earthworms

When I was a little kid, I used to love watching fallen leaves fold up like tiny handkerchiefs, eventually disappearing underground. Watching this now, I know the soil is lively, healthy, and these best friends in nature play a fascinating role in the garden.

They will eat, digest, and excrete food for soil as well as perform all sorts of other useful tasks such as creating passageways for roots to follow. All the while oozing slime that holds up intricate walls for insects to live and move about in.

We're told that worms are so valuable that humans would cease to exist without them. After thirty years of observation, Charles Darwin announced that earthworms can produce half a ton of castings an acre. That's a lot of fertilizer.

Earthworms can live as deep as a meter underground, eating soil as they push their way relentlessly forward or down. Then the bacteria that exist in their guts work away on the material. Anything not digested properly is excreted. Just how much these bacteria do afterward is open to speculation.

Other bacteria are produced to work away on the castings. The result is material rich in nitrogen, potassium, and phosphorus which otherwise comes to us in expensive little bags of fertilizer. Worms do it for free.

We can't even pretend to understand the intricacies of this mechanism. But we do know that the minute we start to fiddle with the soil, or pour chemicals over it, the worm is likely to turn and flee towards a safer haven.

Grass

I deeply resent grass. Wrong. It's not grass, but what grass does to people. It can be a lovely element in a garden, refreshing to walk or play on, it can be a cooling agent and it can also add to the plants that supply us with oxygen.

What I don't like is the pressure it exerts to create perfection. I know people who couldn't care less about nature in any form. But they long for the Perfect Lawn and will spend big bucks on keeping it mowed, fed, dethatched, weeded. And green.

When I ripped out the grass in my own garden, people thought I was a bit of a nutter. "You're the garden lady who hates grass." Not really, it's the practise of feeding and watering grass when all else is going into dormancy during a summer drought that's so calamitous. Grass also strikes me as boring: inert, bereft of sound, rather dull. I hate the machines that break what little quiet we have in the city. But most of all I hate the chemical fertilizers used on lawns.

To feed grass requires lots of compost and manure several times a year, but that won't make perfect grass. And the depletion of the soil below means a lot of work has to go into this unnatural growth. Then constant mowing is required to keep it flawless.

Everywhere I see signs saying Do Not Walk on Grass Sprayed with such and such poison. We're told that tests show that very little of this will come off on the paws of animals, or children's feet. Very little? How about none.

Why don't people see the link between the lawn chemicals and the allergies our children develop? At least we should be thinking about it. A non-chemical lawn probably won't be perfect; it isn't in nature, but it's not a terrible thing either.

Digging

One day I stopped digging. It's like quitting smoking; you have to do it cold turkey. Digging is an addiction. If it was possible, I'd have been digging things up all winter long. No matter where we live, digging is something gardeners *do*.

I love to put things in, then dig them out and put them somewhere else. You might think this is a make-work kind of thing but I feel good and it does the plants no end of wonders. At least they never get too big.

I'm still addicted to that. I'm referring, however, to digging around plants — cultivating. All the books recommend it. It keeps weeds out, they say. But I started contemplating the nature of soil.

We really don't know much about soil. We do know that its structure is so enormously complicated, we've barely begun to analyze this richest part of the biosphere. When I started thinking about the worms making passages for other animals and insects, right down to the microflora and fauna completely unknown to us, I began to realize that digging wasn't a really good idea at all. Surely I was unnecessarily messing up a series of very complicated life forms.

Since I was letting fallen leaves lie, not rushing about tidying up and thinking like a forest, why not extend that? Why dig? It didn't make sense. My feeling now is that I was making myself more useful than I needed to. It's called meddling and I try not to. At least not in the soil.

Paths

I like to think about paths. This seemingly minor thing can create a garden of immeasurable beauty with the right placement, or trivialize another by its banality. My garden is criticized for being too *difficult* to get through. There are no discernible paths among the checkerboard squares. The path through the woodland was formed of its own volition around the berm. You can't race through without spraining an ankle or, worse, bending a plant. But that was my intention. Why run through a garden at all?

We seem to make paths two ways: dead straight to reach a goal as swiftly as possible; or bobbling about for effect but no special reason. Neither appeal to me very much, though I often appreciate a nice straight path wide enough for two people to walk along in comfortable companionship.

I've talked to park designers who say one valuable method of planning is to watch where people walk before they install paths — it tells them how people will use the space. They know where the shortcuts will be before they begin.

Most of the time I don't like a path that meanders for no reason. I can see everything it holds, it has no secrets, and is usually unlovely. Why is it there at all? On the other hand, I do like one that's been mown from a meadow where things are growing up all around and I'm not sure where I'm going. This path has mystery.

Paths that make their way through shrubs so that you aren't quite sure what's beyond them are filled with enchantment. So are paths that angle off into secret places, that lead to soft places to sit and think. It's the path that slows you down, the one that makes you stop to smell the flowers that's the very best one to make.

Le jardin de refusé

There is an area right at the back of the garden that I've dubbed my *jardin de refusé*. It's a play on the phrase *salon de refusé* that artists used to set up in opposition to the academicians accepted by the establishment.

This is where anything that doesn't immediately fit anywhere else in the garden is shoved in summarily and allowed to grow at its own pace. Nothing much is demanded except that it hold masses of plants.

Over the years this excellent concept has changed its function. It's become a nursery garden; a place where I can experiment in small takes and move plants to what might be considered more important parts of the garden.

Rather than looking like a leftover, this small area is often the best looking part of the garden. I like to put giant plants in here to see how fast they will spread or if they can be used where I might need some height.

I like mucking about with different plant combinations. You know after a year if it's going to work. By then, naturally, I become reluctant to change them because they look so good together and so perfect here.

This place looks unruly in spring. I dig up all the tulips from other parts of the garden and toss them in helter-skelter. All the other left-over bulbs somehow find a home here and the foliage mess lingers on and on. But it makes me happy just being in this boisterous place. In spring perhaps I'm not so rigid about what the plants should be doing for me.

Music and the garden

An unwritten rule in our neighborhood holds that you don't play music out of doors. Whenever some fool does, at least ten people rush outside waving their fists. The noise stops.

This is a good rule. I don't want your rock and roll and you probably don't want to listen to my jazz or opera. The idea that it's okay to impose your taste on everyone else came along with the boom boxes kids carry around. "I want noise!" they proclaim.

I don't know how this rule evolved. When we first moved onto the street the whole area was fluid, it was a stopgap on the way to the suburbs, street after street of rooms for rent. Now it's a solid middle-class place where the fences have come down in the front gardens and noise abatement has become a habit.

This simple banning of just one element of city noise makes our streets relatively quiet. Is that why we have so many birds and animals?

There are exceptions, like the young man training to be a singer. We could hear him do his vocal exercises over and over and over. Because it was a fine voice employing regular patterns, it didn't bother anyone. We hoped he'd get a job someday.

Then there is the annual garden party down the street. The first time this happened, it was electrifying. The quiet of a sunny spring afternoon was shattered by a most triumphant sound — a brass quartet playing Bach.

I rushed to the roof to see this in action. "Come over" was the response. So every year we take our wine and our chairs and sit in a neighbor's garden, listening to music that expresses the splendor of being here.

Comfort of the garden

For a couple of weeks, a few years ago, I didn't know what kind of cancer I had. It might be very serious, or not. We had to wait for tests. After you stop crying, you wander into the garden. Everything in this period was incredibly poignant. *What ifs* started flowing through my mind. What if this was the last May I would spend here? What if I can't spend the summer here? What if I die?

I understand now why cancer patients see life with incredible intensity. Each day is a rejoicing. To be alive is almost good enough. Each flower, each leaf has some special message in it. A message of pleasure as well as succor.

I spent most of those weeks trying to be normal but knowing nothing was normal. Not in the feelings I had for everyone around me (I am lucky to have lots of friends as well as family). I worked on yoga every day, and I tried to meditate and to imagine the alien cells in my body as things that had to be uprooted and thrown out.

Cancer cells are black and ugly. I saw them on the monitor in the oncologist's examining room. So I had a vision of what I wanted to get rid of. Great, dark, interloping, fast-breeding invasive plants that you'd whack out the minute you'd come upon them. I could find no equivalent plant in nature to help with this visualization. Nothing seemed as bad or destructive.

I was elated when the news came through that it had been removed successfully. But I also lost something — an edge, a way of looking. I remember the unvarnished intensity and specialness of those few weeks. And now I know that we should all try to live with the knowledge a cancer patient understands profoundly of how glorious it is to be alive.

Attitude

A great deal of gardening is about attitude. When I look at chewed up leaves I think, Somebody's getting a good meal, rather than, Get me the spray, there's a pest in here! If it bothers me, I take off my glasses and go about nearsightedly peering at the world with my usual blurry vision — a world that has no hard edges.

I used to try to keep my attitude benign, feeling there was enough death in the garden without my adding to it. But then I never used to be able to even get near a bug. This cringing attitude has changed. I can kill anything I don't like (earwigs, for instance) without a shudder. I can pick up slugs and hold them, letting them slime all over my hands without a *frisson*.

I have learned not to move the furniture on the deck until I've checked that all the spiders have moved their webs. If they haven't, things stay as they are until they get sick of my moving around and wind upwards to a more peaceful spot. I used to be petrified of spiders but now I see them as efficient bug catchers.

The stingers — wasps and bees — used to hold sheer terror for me. Now they are pollinators helping to make my garden the rich source of enjoyment it is. I just brush by them making as little motion as possible so as not to disturb.

And the infestations that come along occasionally to upset the rhythms of the garden — these I leave knowing that the aphids and their little herders, the ants, will mean that ladybugs will sense there's a feast here. They will obliterate them without any help from me at all. Over the years I've found that the garden has much to teach, especially if I keep an open mind.

Working with nature

The idea of working with nature, accepting what it actually offers, took root very early on in my gardening life. It came instinctively and is at the core of the way I like to work. Some through osmosis, some from sheer laziness, and a great deal by observation.

I knew immediately that this garden was part of a larger scheme of things, not just a personal oasis. I never saw my little spread as being isolated from what was growing nearby.

I couldn't cut down the eighty-foot weeping willow in my neighbor's garden, but I could find plants that would be happy to grow all around it. I could put a compost under its shallow roots to make new food for everything else in the garden.

It gave me a chance to find out all the new things that might thrive here; to have plants for attracting insects I hadn't seen for a long time — butterflies being my main interest. The more and various plants I put in, the more birds and insects came to stay. So did the hummingbirds. They didn't come to drink out of a plastic bottle but from the plants whose blossoms they can sip nectar from.

When I contemplate how much land we gardeners own, abutting each other as we do, without thinking of the power we have at our fingertips, I wonder why we don't organize. We could become a powerful lobby to protect the environment. Thinking about gardens in a larger context is something all gardeners will eventually have to come to if humanity is to survive.

Looking at gardens

I n yoga there are exercises to keep the eyes sharp and limber even into old age. The same can be said of looking at gardens. This makes a lively aesthetic and keeps it evolving. Creative stealing of garden concepts is a perfectly respectable pursuit in gardening. Once you've applied them to your own space, filtered them through your own mind, what's left of them anyway? How different from stealing someone else's ideas, or phrases, or taking away something of another's personality by co-opting a mannerism.

In gardening, filching a plant combination is always prefaced with "So and so had this, now I'm trying it." But everyone else's context is so completely different, the original owner would probably never recognize the theft at first glance.

This is why I love to show pictures of where I might have stolen an idea from and then the result in my own garden. For one thing, it's never as good as the original (we gardeners are perpetually modest). But, in time, it reflects my taste. And someone else will come along and think it worthy enough to be lifted into their own gardens. And so the cycle reverberates onward.

For those who start out visually challenged, looking at other people's gardens tones the eye, makes it more discriminating. It teaches how not to be bamboozled by flashy effect. It means learning to trust that eye by filtering out the worst and finding the best in every garden.

Every garden has a virtue. Where is it? What is it? What can be taken away and reused? You can always learn something by peering into someone else's life. And into their gardens.

Points of view

The developer who looks at a field and sees it as an empty place is the same person who sees a rushing stream flinging itself, unused, into the sea — and believes it is going to waste because it hasn't been harnessed or sold for profit.

This kind of thinking has dominated the public mind for so long we've lost contact with what the field and the stream are actually doing. Otherwise why would we cover over prime growing land with parking lots and shopping malls? And why would we divert rivers to accommodate the bureaucrats and engineers?

What an ecologist sees is not an empty field but a home for butterflies, wildflowers, and a sanctuary for animals and insects on the run from civilization. The stream provides valuable breeding ground for fish. It cleanses and purifies the air around.

I wish the developers, the saviors of sacrosanct jobs, would get together with environmentalists. It's terrifying that being an ecologically minded person is equated with being a desperado for the earth who is egocentric and uncaring about other people.

Why isn't there room for both points of view? Extremists on both sides say outrageous things. But what's most important is that we have a planet left to exploit and pull profits from for the next generation. This is a fact which seems to evade a great many of those who want to cut down the forests and dam the waterways.

That's why gardening is important. It is a small step towards understanding how intricately things are meshed together. It teaches us how one plant depends on another and, ultimately, how we are utterly dependent on plants for our very survival.

Time

I am the person you can set your clock by. I once arrived at a restaurant fifteen minutes late — and even the maître d' was ready to call hospitals. If you invite me to your brunch at 12:30, that's when I'll arrive.

I picked up this habit of punctuality from my parents of course. Our house ran on schedules. At 9 a.m. there was Sunday school. At 10 a.m. there was choir practise. At 11 a.m. there was church service. Between one and two, there was Sunday dinner, and so on. We were never late to anything without being scolded severely. Being a dreamy little kid, I learned about time the hard way.

When I started to garden seriously, I set schedules. Schedules that were thrown out almost immediately. No one can garden for an hour, anymore than they can go into the garden for a few minutes.

Since this is an activity that consumes the whole body, takes over the mind and intrudes upon the soul, where does time fit in? Almost nowhere at all. My sense of time now is measured in a very different way than hours.

It has become measurable in areas, jobs to do, things to plant. I make no promises about where I'll be when the weather is particularly good. I'm likely to be in the garden until it's done. This plays hell with being a writer. Because that's as obsessional as gardening and these two parts of my life vie for my attention every waking hour. But I will still arrive maddeningly on time if you invite me to your party.

The toolshed

I took it into my mind to check out the toolshed. It's really a junk shed. What's needed is in front, whatever archaeological accretion builds up behind is lost to human view. Forever.

This was certainly true of our shed. And it reflected how completely my garden information had changed over the years. At the very back there was a container of Cygon-2, a potent bug killer, purchased when I bought the birch tree. "The tree won't survive," I was told, "unless you spray it with this chemical. It will get the birch borer." I dutifully plunked down my money.

But when I read the instructions it sounded lethal not to just the birch borer but almost everything else. I stuck it unopened into the back, never to see the light of day until now. It's noxious to almost everything (especially birch borers). Though the poison was never used, the birch appears to be thriving all by itself. I make sure it has enough sun, that there's water in really dry periods. The fact that I planted a native and not a European birch also had a great deal to do with the lack of birch borers.

Then there was an almost full container of glysophate. Now this is a herbicide that doesn't accumulate in the soil, has a short life, and breaks down quickly. It kills systemically. I guess I never found enough weeds that I hate systemically enough to want to kill because it's long since lost any potency.

The Toxic Taxi took these things away. And it bothers me. I'm not sure we should be buying anything that we can't dispose of easily. Or that even needs special disposal.

Slugs

I do go on about my great love of nature. But there are things I positively loathe about it as well. Slugs, for instance. I'm sure there's a reason for their existence but it escapes me most days.

I get up at the crack of dawn on slug patrol. I'm so inured to their sliming that I can pick dozens up with bare hands and stomp on them with relish. It certainly gets the adrenaline up to speed. A fine way to start the day.

I've tried all sorts of ways to get rid of them. Folk methods, stuff I've made up myself. But experience tells me there is really only one effective way: pick them off and kill them one by one. It's mucky but cheap.

Buying slug bait may suit some people. But you have to cover any dead slugs with lime or salt so that birds won't swoop down and eat them. The bait will get into the bird's digestive system, affect their egg production. One thing leads inevitably to another.

You can trap slugs with horseradish plants — but you'll have to scrape them off the leaves at dawn to get rid of them. You can plant mustard around the edge of the garden again but you still have to get them off in the morning and throw them into a pot of salt.

I've used ground ginger, salt lines, and, more recently, edged borders with rock powder. It's worth almost anything that's not toxic to get rid of slugs. If you get mad enough in the garden maybe you'll end up inventing something new.

Squirrels

The chestnut planted by the steps had grown into a tall stick with fairly large leaves before I even spotted it. It was planted by a squirrel.

Most of the time I find myself hating squirrels. "Tree rats," as a hort-buddy calls them. The north side of the garden supports the grayish red squirrels, the south side the black ones. They have their own territory and though they cross back and forth, each seems to respect the other's turf.

They are sent to drive me insane. I plant, they pull up. Narcissus may be poisonous to them but that doesn't mean they can't be hauled out for a good look. The same goes for all the other bulbs they are curious about and don't deign to eat.

I know they are part of a system that requires them to bring seeds and nuts into the garden for the survival of future generations of plants and animals. But I wish I had some say in this.

To anyone not used to a squirrel's outrageous behavior, they must seem enchanting. They dart about the trees chasing one another playfully. They are bold as can be — coming right up to the house if they think there's food about.

One of my hort-gurus leaves enough food in the garden so that the squirrels will leave her bulbs alone and let the garden be. She is convinced that this is true. She certainly had me convinced until she told me that they would tap on the window when there wasn't any food available. Maybe I'll just leave nature to find its own way about how to forage rather than giving it a hand.

Plants for bugs

O f all the many wonders of gardening, one of the most satisfying is planting to attract the kind of bugs that will keep the garden clean. Supposing there's an infestation of aphids — tiny creatures marching lockstep up and down tender stems, sucking the life out of them. Herded about by ants who love them for the nectar they ooze from their little bottoms. They kill swiftly.

Angelica, dill, and fennel, all great herbs in themselves graced with alluring foliage, will bring in ladybugs. Ladybugs in turn will eat aphids. Once the aphids disappear the ants will probably lower their population and stop being pests.

Achillea or yarrow, tansy, and White Sensation cosmos are plants that look gorgeous in combination with Queen Anne's lace. They will also attract all the right bugs. Add a bit of water and perhaps a place for them to shelter — something enticing such as a nice shrub or two.

There's another benefit here too. Butterflies. Queen Anne's lace will attract black swallowtail; anise, the swallowtail butterfly. Add a few of the simply gorgeous autumn asters and you will have painted ladies. And if you love the fritillary, add some violas to the mix.

Then there are annuals like the helichrysum that some moths love beyond all others. The larvae are laid in the soft felt of the leaves and spin their comforting protective web. Before I knew a living creature was developing in this benign net, I used to cut all these "infested" leaves off to get rid of them. Now I watch in total fascination waiting for the day when I will actually see them hatch.

The old lilac

When we moved into the house in 1967 there wasn't much here except fence-to-fence weeds and an ancient lilac bush with one bloom on it. This poor, ratty, old shrub was slashed almost to death.

That weary lilac bush taught me a lot about gardening. I had never owned a garden before, never cared for a plant. The lilac became my fifth child. I carefully cut off the solitary bloom, trimmed out all the dead wood (I knew enough to recognize you should do that), and waited to see what would happen.

The next year more blossoms appeared, and I did more pruning. I even bought a good pair of secateurs to do it with. I wasn't afraid of this plant because I thought if I kill it, that's okay since it was free. Still, it became a kind of mission.

How to make the lilac look better, feel better, and give me a glorious June bouquet? I removed all the suckers, cut back anything that looked stringy or ugly, any shoots that poked out of the sides where I didn't want them. I bought a saw and took off a huge section that was dead. I gave it buckets of bonemeal. We even cut a chunk out of the deck to make it more comfortable.

The following year, it was covered in blooms. I rushed around opening up doors and windows. Its scent filled the whole house, *my* lilac was reincarnated.

Summer

The scents of summer

What a glorious time of year the height of summer is. The perfumes that rise in the early evening air are intoxicating — nicotiana opens up to attract the moths that do their pollinating in the evening. Evening stock, ipomoea, four-o'clocks empty their bouquet into the garden just as we like to sit outside with a glass of wine.

But the days have not been neglected. When it's brushed accidentally or its foliage is crushed, *Helichrysum angustifolium* exudes the pungent scent of its common name — curry plant.

Lavenders, artemisias, and caryopteris have their distinctive sage-like aroma that grow more and more intense the hotter it becomes.

Butterflies and moths depend far more on smell than bees. They will seek out such aromatic plants as honeysuckle, daphne, and buddleias. But it's the species of a plant family that butterflies are attracted to. The flowers aren't as large as more exotic hybrids, but plant them, and *voilà*, the butterflies will come.

Bees have a kind of ultraviolet vision to see blossoms for their own use. Being lured into buying a plant because it has super double blooms may only appeal to you and not to the insects that yearn to drink its nectar.

More and more insects arrive with a greater variety of scents and colors in the garden. Species evolve specifically for the best they have to offer insects and animals. Not something mankind has messed about with.

Plant rhythms

Nothing captures a child's attention like a plant's habit of moving its head towards the sun. Heliotropism wasn't lost on me when I was a young one. I'd check out the sunflower in my Victory garden plot after school, at noon and four, to see where its head was.

I didn't know it was called heliotropism until we learned all the different parts of the plants and their functions in our science class.

It's taken almost half a century but scientists are just now beginning to understand what makes up the biological rhythms of a plant. They've discovered a gene that controls the movement of a plant, its time of bloom, when the leaves move, even when the pores open. It is miraculous, invisible.

Plants, like people, have masses of energy very early in the morning so they can face the day. Will scientists eventually find out that plants, like people, get depressed? That they have emotions of fear and love? That they can signal warnings to one another when an enemy approaches?

We know that talking to plants helps them to grow but that's because we exhale the carbon dioxide they need. We know that certain kinds of music (usually classical) make them grow faster.

What we don't know is how much all of this will help us to survive in the future. In fact, our very dependence on plants may be far greater than we've suspected up to now. Plants hold the secrets to many things. Look at them with respect. Plants, like a lot of people, may take a long time to reveal their secrets.

Summer storm

No one notices weather in the city unless there's a disaster: a freak electrical storm that downs all the lights; a tornado that blasts through destroying everything in its path; or a hurricane where no hurricane has gone before.

We have no control over the weather, so we who live in the city do our best to ignore it. We're irritated when a summer brunch is rained out. The weather report didn't predict this. But of course if we'd looked at the western horizon (supposing we could see the horizon), we'd have noticed the clouds roiling up into dark and angry balls filled with rain.

We used to always know what the weather was by reading the signs: pigs rooting about restlessly before a storm, leaves twisting a certain way before a heavy downpour. But we've forgotten our connection with the elements. We've distanced ourselves from another performance by nature.

I remember attending a garden party held under a large canopy. Very elegant with mounds of strawberries and clotted cream. I looked towards the western sky to see huge black clouds forming so quickly I said to my friend, "We've got about five minutes to get out of here or we're going to be drenched."

Less than ten minutes later we were in the car and it was raining so hard we had to pull over and wait until the storm had passed. We sat exhilarated, pleased to have missed being soaked. The sky is the best predictor of weather and I don't mind taking my chances with a few old sayings either.

Relearning the senses

One of the things our grandson, Nick, learned very early was how to sniff. He had observed people sniffing flowers and imitated them when he saw a flower represented in a book.

The first spring of his life was filled with long meandering walks, his nose poked into any plant en route. He sniffed the cotoneaster that sits at the edge of the front garden (I checked — no distinct scent); he worked hard on the artemisias which he finds not greatly to his liking. I steered him away from the roses — not yet.

Next he discovered touching plants. He loved to crush flowers in his tiny hands. It feels so good, who could resist? But that gradually changed into stroking the leaves of lamb's ears (*Stachys lanata*), or feeling the sage plant with its rough surface.

Then he began to distinguish all the colors he saw in the garden. He named reds, blues, yellows as his favorites.

Detecting ants, spiders, or anything scuttling along on the ground brings him to a dead halt for a long stare. He's been trained not to step on them or to meddle, just observe. His attention span, about fifteen seconds, will improve with age.

So far he hasn't been tempted to taste the garden but that too will come. And then he'll have to learn what's poisonous (aconitum), what will hurt (rose thorns), and what's safe to stick in the mouth (daisy petals).

As he learned to use his senses, Nick taught us to do the same. Sometimes we need to inhabit the skin of a small child to revitalize our own sensual selves.

Gardeners and bugs

I squash bugs, stomp on slugs, cut and hack at the garden. And yet I think of myself as a mild-mannered person, not prone to violence. But just let something threaten my plants. I get mean.

Take the asparagus beetle — please. This is a fascinating insect. I'd never even seen one until I put in a couple of lines of asparagus. The minute they were allowed to turn into ferns, these strange and beautiful beetles showed up unheralded.

I spent hours looking at them through a magnifying glass. They have a very interesting sex life and don't seem to mind voyeurs at all. The broad back has diamonds on it and they go through an exotic gavotte before actually mounting. At least I think that's what's going on.

Then, the next thing I knew, my asparagus plants, by now lovely ephemeral wands, had this revolting sticky black stuff all over them. The larval form of the bug, I discovered. Not quite the gossamer effect I had in mind.

I took them off by hand but it was a yucky business even for one not squeamish. Nothing would do except heavy spraying with soapy water and a good shower.

I'm also perfectly happy to bump off earwigs any way I can. They have fierce pincers and you know it when they bite. They will also cheerfully come into the house but I prefer my bugs out of doors.

The garden can bring out the best and the worst in us. But in this case, I think the violence is more than acceptable.

Stopping to read

One summer my life was in such a turmoil, I stopped reading. I read on trains, in cars, even on the street. Always have. But that year, I found reading too painful, each word had such emotive qualities, it sent me into despair. So I stopped. And the year of not reading was radical.

I found I could remember poetry. It bubbled up from deep pools to the surface of my mind, poetry I hadn't read for many years. I could recall whole novels, movies, paintings not thought about for years. I kept going deeper into the wellspring of memory.

I learned to sit still during this year. This is especially difficult when you're a person on the move constantly, doing things for most hours of every day. I think this must be hardest for women — to stop looking after people, to give up what control we have over their lives. To stop feeling responsible all the time.

Stopping to sit still, to do nothing, to not feel useful. It was devastating. I had to train myself to sit and stare and to let my mind run freely. It took months to accomplish this. It was like going back to childhood when I was allowed to roam over the hills or to be in the lake for hours without having to account for time. What was I thinking about then? What was I thinking about now?

I started hearing the sounds around me rather than have my mind cluttered up with information all the time. I heard my neighborhood instead of cutting it out to withdraw into myself. I learned to look carefully. I saw line and form where I'd seen nothing before. And once again I fell in love with where I was living and who I was living with.

A changed outlook

When I learned to stop living in busyness, and learned to sit still, to think quietly, I found I had the means close at hand to actually change my life.

What began to form in my mind was that I must not only change the way I was living but how I was living. I changed the house, then turned my thoughts to the garden. It was a neglected thing that had never been made much of. That's where the real change began and it altered the timbre of my whole life.

I remember telling an acquaintance that I'd become an obsessed gardener. "Aha," he said, "the children have left home, you've turned fifty, and you're going through the menopause."

I hated that man. "Two out of three," I replied cryptically. The children *had* left home and I had become mistress of my own yard once again. But making the decision to create a garden wasn't a substitute for missing children or turning menopausally inward. It was the choice to use almost everything I'd ever learned and fashion something completely new. That fundamental decision changed my life.

The garden became a metaphor for what beauty there could be in an unpromising place. How I could mold things in a creative way. It was something I could do totally alone without consultation. In other words, it showed me the way to freedom from a city life that was becoming unendurable.

Skunks

Thoreau calls the fox, the skunk, and the rabbit "Nature's watchmen — links which connect the day of animated life." They start their rambles at night, covering their own territory, foraging.

I could smell our skunk long before a sighting was made. Sometimes I would lie in bed in the very early morning and move my head in tandem smelling him as he walked along the alley way.

My neighbor was walking her dog at dawn. The dog ran over to a bag of garbage and got hit straight in the face by skunk juice. All the traditional remedies were used: tomato juice, letting the poor beast run round and round their yard. The whole area reeked for days. I kind of liked it.

I don't find skunk smell offensive. But then I like the smell of manure as well. It seems to me that they are as close to natural odors as we're going to get in the city and if we can get them unvarnished, intense, that's fine with me.

And using Thoreau's romantic notion of them as the links between the life of the night and life of the day makes our local skunk even more valuable. I want to know more about my skunk. Where does he sleep during the day? What does he eat? There is something so touching about the wildlife that still manages to live beside us. And I revere them for it. They are the true survivors.

Picking a bouquet of flowers

The first time anyone cut flowers in my garden I was on a long-distance call and couldn't yell "Stop that!" It's not that this is such a composed scene each plant has a part to play in the overall picture (there are gardens like that). It's that I just never dreamed of it as a place to harvest flowers for the house.

I'm sure there must be a Platonic form somewhere that says you never pick flowers in other people's gardens. But my friend didn't know this and she didn't know my unspoken rule about not felling flowers for the vase.

I didn't even know I had the rule until I saw these blooms appear indoors. I was distraught beyond anything that the situation demanded. And felt embarrassed by my own anxiety.

I set about to correct the situation. I put in a small area strictly for cutting. I could have all the flowers I wanted for arrangements in three seasons and still have lots left over.

It doesn't take much space. A few square feet and some divisions of shasta daisies, a couple of roses, coreopsis, mallows, garlic chives, and so on. But soon this little area took on a life of its own. I moved plants around so that they related better to each other. Added more, started expanding the palette until it looked so good I didn't want to cut anything down for the house.

So I have a garden full of flowers and nothing to bring indoors. I let the flowers live where they should — outside.

Contrasts

I can't believe the contrast between today and yesterday. Then it was teeming with rain so thick and wet that you couldn't see across the road. Clouds seemed to rest on the face of the earth and we were shrouded in mists.

Today the sun is again shining brilliantly. It's as though the planet has been scrubbed clean. Gone are the dog droppings from the road, washed away is the dust and dirt of civilization. We are clean and new again. And the air is filled with a brio that seem to lift the spirits and make them soar.

But what a good old soggy day does is help you to feel really sorry for yourself. If the world is to be depressed, so am I. Novelists call this pathetic fallacy. It's pathetic to think that the weather, the light, that even the temperature reflects our moods as we look out into the gloomy mist. But we pathetic humans like to think we're the center of the universe and it is ours to direct — even moodily.

I never avoid a good depression on a particularly wet day. I like to read poetry and doodle in a notebook but I don't think about going outside.

It's the contrast that I like when the weather lifts. Life gives us an enormous variety of joys but this is one of the great gifts: coming out of the gloom into the sun again. We humans do like to suffer and, with the right frame of mind, sometimes it's almost enjoyable.

The dog days of summer

A heat wave, we're told, is any three successive days with temperatures of around 32°C. Everything is stifling, the humidity is unbearable. I can't move plants around — too dangerous for them — which puts me in a grumpy frame of mind.

It is during this kind of weather that I get really upset about the nitwits who water their lawns. They usually do it at high noon, losing most of it to evaporation anyway.

People do a lot of things to their gardens automatically. Watering lawns is one of those activities. Maybe because it doesn't require any thought. But watering should be an art.

I like to get up just before sunrise, killing slugs and figuring out where I should hand water. I have a wonderful old watering can with a long spout that makes this more like fun than a chore. And in this cool light just before the city roars to life, I feel blissfully alone with my plants. I creep about giving long drinks to those plants that need it most — the ones with the big fleshy leaves. These are the indicator plants. If they are wilting, everything around them will surely be parched.

The pots are all gathered into one spot with no thought given to aesthetics. They are watered en masse in the morning and again in the evening and I give them as much protection as I can. Water is like so many other essentials in our lives, we cannot, must not, take it for granted.

The silver maple

The silver maple's vast root system bolts its way through my garden, scooping up nutrients, breaking up the sewage system. I see a tree that should be in a forest, not a city. But my guest from Wales stood in awe of this tree, amazed by its bark, its graceful canopy. My neighbor planted a silver maple against our mutual fence. I mourned for my garden. But he loves his silver maple and the law says you can plant anything you want on your own property. I certainly didn't consult him when I put in a dozen trees, and the more than one hundred shrubs. It was a bugbear between us for years.

And I think about a friend who also lives next to a silver maple. A whole colony of them unchecked, unpruned. A branch the size of a normal tree hung over her garden. One day it came crashing down. The most terrifying part of this was not that it destroyed a very large wooden deck, but that her husband had been sitting there seconds before. He could have been killed at worst, maimed at best.

The whole concept of stewardship seems to come to a definite halt when considering trees. I wonder if people give any thought at all to how their plants will affect those around them. Do they think about the root systems, shade, what makes a plant invasive or even dangerous in the city? I doubt it. We are very selfish when it comes to our own property. If we *are* going to plant silver maples, these monarchs of the forest, we'd better be willing to take long-term responsibility for whatever havoc they can inflict.

Plant culture

You keep hearing about mall culture and business culture as though there were all sorts of magical properties connected with hanging out at the mall or going to the office. They are supposed to have an ethic, values, certain mode of behavior, a certain way of living to comprise this culture.

Well, there really is a plant culture. And it's far more serious. It's what the plant needs to grow on. How many hours of sun, the absolute minimum amount of water for survival, and what kind of soil it needs in order to thrive.

These are all important but origin is even more significant in plant culture. If it comes from Europe, it will most likely be a plant that's happy to live in the eastern part of the continent. If it comes from Asia or from Australia, it might do best in the northwest of the continent. Though these are by no means rules.

The origin can also tell you a lot about the other things about plant culture. One from the mountains is sure to be one that lies closer to the ground, likes very sharp drainage, and can take high winds. If it comes from a maritime region, it will be able to withstand both wind and salt air. A desert plant is most likely to have hairs on its surface to capture and hold moisture from the dewy morning air.

Plant culture comes from a great deal of observation and knowledge and yet it only begins to scratch the surface of any plant's complicated life. Somehow I don't think mall culture competes.

Damaging the soil

Gardeners like to rabbit on about what they fertilize the garden with. How they get rid of unwanted insects and diseases. But when you raise the subject of just how much this all costs, nobody wants to confess how expensive it is. We've been brainwashed into thinking that we *must* use these items or we aren't being conscientious gardeners.

This has always struck me as being a bit daft. But then maybe I'm a skinflint. What did people do before the chemical industry got in on the agribusiness and convinced farmers that they needed the magic bullet of chemical fertilizers to increase their yield?

At the time — the end of World War II — no one talked about the health of the soil, or what these things were doing to soil, mainly because no one knew. Mass chemical dependence was set up.

How do you tell a farmer or a gardener who's been using the same methods for twenty or thirty years that they are probably harmful? You'll get an answer something like: "Okay, but what about all these bugs and other infestations that we have to deal with?" The answer is that if we hadn't started using these alleged bits of magic, maybe we wouldn't have the other things that seem to be attendant on them.

It's increasingly obvious that the old ways of tending to nature's needs, and not imposing the latest in technology, might contain the wisdom we've been ignoring for too long. You hear that we can't turn back the clock. Why not? We may have to if we want to recover the ravaged soil we're passing on to the next generation.

Cancer and the garden

I have a friend with a serious form of cancer. She has been through the medical wars — chemotherapy, radiation, weird diets — tested to a fare-thee-well. But she turned her back on all that and put her face to the garden. When she found out how her life would change, she decided to make a new garden.

She tore out a stand of the dreaded Chinese elm, releasing a huge area of the garden. She raised beds to make it easier to get at her digging and weeding. She mixed and matched and moved. She was undaunted by the assault on her body. And friends could only be awed by her courage and her extraordinary sense of future.

In went trees that she'd fallen in love with. A ginkgo, linden, *Magnolia stellata*, hemlock. And shrubs like viburnum, witch hazel, oak-leaf hydrangea, sea buckthorn, enkianthus. Hundreds of bulbs and dozens of perennials in dazzling colors.

Though she's been through the dark night of her own body and soul, she's been a radiant presence that makes you especially proud of being a gardener. There haven't been long complaints about the poisons roiling in her body. It's been: "You should see what I put in the garden today. It's incredible."

The garden has been her way of hanging on to that remarkably profound desire to stay alive, to be the very best while going through the very worst. She says it's her intoxication: "To dote over a tiny flourishing plant magically released me from the prison of my own fear and gently reconnected me to the much-loved wonder of the sensual world." It's something those of us who know her keep in mind now.

Secret places

Every garden must have secrets. More than just little surprises when you turn a corner. But real secrets. Our garden is filled with secret graves — mice, rabbits, cats, birds (lots of birds).

I had a friend who is partly North American Indian. When her adored cat died, I watched as she spilled out her grief in the cold autumn light. She dug a small hole, which faced north and south, and put the little shoe box filled with one of her favorite T-shirts and the kitty. She placed it tenderly in the hole, covered it lightly with soil, and then burned a small pile of sweetgrass, waving its smoke upward, to show her respect for the animal and its death.

I think about that cat every time I go near the spot and wonder if her soul is wandering about anywhere. All the birds and mice and gerbils that died were also buried in shoe boxes and had little ceremonies to go along with them. The worst was burying the turtle and then hearing this eerie scratching as we were about to inter the body. We'd forgotten they hibernate when it gets cold. Out came the turtle.

There are other secrets in the garden. Little groups of shells and stones that I rearrange each year so that the worms won't bury them. Some of these are gifts from people and I like to have them nearby as remembrances. Others are just lovely things that I am enchanted to find when I lift a leaf or move a branch.

Some days I am overwhelmed by the feeling of all those other secrets that this garden holds that were planted and left behind long before even I was born. There is a continuity here.

Espalier

I love to prune, and a little creative cutting never hurt most plants of my acquaintance. But I'm uncomfortable with bonsai and I don't like topiary. The practise of cutting away at plants to keep them a certain size or shape doesn't fit in with my aesthetic. I hate seeing plants shaped like bunnies or even balls. They should look like plants, not aspire to something they aren't.

But I do admire a fine bit of espalier. This was invented for small city gardens. Trained up against a sheltering wall, plants can make not only a beautiful design but grow fruit as well.

The great pride of my friend John's garden is an espaliered pear tree which covers all of one wall. He's done a splendid job of pruning and even manages to get fruit from this small space.

Until he read a book on pruning, that is. He was following the dotted line scrupulously and cut it back so hard it almost died. A few years passed, the pear recovered from the assault and he observes the plant now, leaving books indoors.

Training a plant to move along a wire or a trellis in some simplified design (a chevron, or candelabra) seems just fine. Why one kind of drastic pruning is all right and another is not is puzzling. Bonsai makes me think of foot binding. Animals grown out of ivy and boxwood bring on nausea. But show me something up against a wall and I swoon with delight. Don't ask me to explain the inconsistencies of a gardener.

Tough-love gardening

There are days when I feel I'm a grouch of a gardener. I will pull out a plant if it isn't doing what I want it to do. I will transplant things when all the books say you're not supposed to, if the spirit so moves me.

One of my theories of gardening is that you can do almost anything to a plant and it will probably survive. This doesn't always work, of course. Though I'm not the most patient of gardeners, I can plunk a plant in the ground and it usually grows.

I prune, sometimes not well, but very often. I chop on those black days I need to hack away at living tissue. I call this the hack-and-hope school of pruning. It's not recommended.

I often forget to give my plants water unless there's a terrible drought or they are literally gasping with need. They usually survive on what nature provides — a good thing.

I never feed my plants anything much beyond what the garden itself provides. We have compost here; I get some manure in every year, but mostly it's leaving weeds pulled up on the spot to break down and do their job of feeding plants.

Where all of this system breaks down is with fussy plants. I insist on them, loving to worry over a few rare beauties that give as much for the hand to do as the eye to absorb.

All of this is on a day when I'm in one of my marching-over-the-face-of-the-land moods. Just don't get in my way. When this passes the garden sighs with relief.

Monarch butterflies

One warm evening, walking about at a friend's place on the huge bluffs that skirt Lake Ontario, I was thunderstruck by the sight of every tree at the edge of the property covered with monarch butterflies. This was part of the legendary butterfly migration I'd heard about but never dreamed of seeing.

The butterflies were on their way north to nesting areas where they lay their young in fields of milkweed — the food supply for a new generation. I wondered, sadly, if there would be any fields of milkweed in a few years. But at that moment I stood stock still gazing at these magnificent creatures.

Every leaf, every inch of stem quivered gently with their life. The light from the late-afternoon sun touched and warmed them as they rested, seeming to breath as one huge mass. They must have stopped here after the long haul across the huge lake, coming up from their wintering grounds in Mexico.

The source of those grounds has been discovered and ecologists feel that it's best to keep it a secret. They are afraid that poachers will come and take them away by the thousands, endangering those left.

I slipped back into the house to get my camera as quickly and quietly as possible. But the others saw I was up to something and came running after me. One woman clapped her hands, yelled sharply, and the whole body of butterflies rose as one and flew off. "Why?" I asked. "I just wanted to see them move," she replied. I know why some of nature's secrets should be kept that way.

The sorority of gardeners

T he sisterhood is definitely powerful in the gardening world. I've made dozens of new friends just belonging to a garden organization. We refer to each other as "new best friends." I happened into this group by sheer good luck.

I was asked to be on the board of a hort organization. It became quite clear that I wasn't going to be great at this. I have a short attention span for meetings. I ritually glazed off. I begged to be released to run a committee. That was a lot more fun because one of the rules is that we wouldn't have meetings, we'd talk on the phone or fax one another.

But being on the board meant that I met this incredible group of dynamic, funny, intelligent, and wildly energetic women. They all seem to run something, have kids, and garden with a passion. We decided to have dinner parties. Just to talk about gardening, ourselves, or whatever was interesting whether it was sex or politics.

I adore these women. And I've found them all over the place. When I go out and speak or travel to look at gardens this little society seems to collect around our passion.

There are lots and lots of men who garden with just as much interest and knowledge but there's no getting together with them on such a spontaneous level, or to be at ease so quickly as a group of women who have at least one interest in common. Do I feel close to them — oh yes. And I would trust them with my soul.

Wind

When I was growing up on the prairies, we memorized a poem called "The Wind Our Enemy" by Ann Marriott. It spoke of the despair a young woman feels as she watches the wind taking away the topsoil, of the desperation of being poor and the loneliness of her life underlined by the unceasing wind.

The rhythms of the poem caught the soughing of the prairie wind for my romantic little being. I'd lie beside a field of wheat so that I could capture that sense of perpetual motion. And I've loved the wind ever since. There is no despair or loneliness there for me. And it has never made me fearful. But then I'm neither sailor nor farmer.

Some winds are soft and caressing, more than a breeze, less than a storm. We don't think much about wind in the middle of the city. It's painful as you walk between huge buildings downtown when the most innocuous stirring of the air turns to a gale. But other buildings provide refuge. Or you go underground.

I hate being away from the wind. Maybe I'm claustrophobic, but it doesn't seem right to me to be underneath miles of concrete.

I love going into the garden when there's a heavy wind to whip the weeping willow into a frenzy. It bends plants almost to the ground taking out the dead and the weak.

One day a huge branch came tumbling down from the dying tree in the neighbor's garden. It was heading straight for our huge back windows when a sudden wind whipped it away from the house and left us safe. I could never think of the wind as an enemy.

The weeping willow

It was once a stick found on the ground by my old neighbor. He shoved it into the earth near our fence some thirty years ago. Now the weeping willow rises to loom more than eighty feet over three gardens apart from its own. Never has a plant had a more forceful personality. And no other plant has so controlled the way I garden. When we first arrived here, it was as enchanting as I could imagine. This graceful little thing, hardly bigger than a shrub, was a real ornament. The next year it was a large tree and then by the fifth year it had turned my sunny garden into a shady one.

The growth of the tree was subtle. In fact I didn't realize just how big it had become until I saw it from several houses away. It looked like a tree in the middle of a park, which is probably where it should have been.

It is the thirstiest of all plants and so is pleased with the situation it finds itself in: with the spring flood and an attentive gardener to make sure that nothing goes completely dry.

For a few years I tried cutting as many branches off my side of the tree without distorting its shape. But then one got away and now the one limb is as big as two trees stretching over my own and into another neighbor's garden, changing the light as it grows.

It is a mammoth presence. I remember standing alone out there waiting for an eclipse of the moon. The wind came up and everything about the tree seemed almost menacing as it swayed with the evening wind.

I can understand how whole populations could come to revere trees or make them into sacred icons given the weeping willow. But that doesn't make me love it one bit more.

Defensive gardening

My neighbor tells me that if I want silence I should move to the country. I don't want to be anywhere other than in my own garden. But on some summer days it's impossible to go outside. It's the dreaded renovators. And our neighborhood is filled with them.

Renovations apparently go on for years. The noise of machines shatter the air and I go crazy. Even the cat doesn't want to lie in the warm sunshine. So I do the next best thing, I wear a huge ear muff-like radio to work outside. I look a bit like an airline pilot but I'm really listening to the opera, to Bach or Bruckner.

These bafflers are just the trick. I'm isolated from some of the noise of the city. I live in hope that all these people will finish before I die and I'll have a few years of quiet left before me.

The other motors that drive me mad are electric mowers. Our neighborhood doesn't have gardens even big enough to justify these machines but people use them anyway. They don't do nearly as good a job as a push mower and take slightly longer. I've never understood the attraction. And the less said about the scourge of leaf blowers the better — surely the silliest invention ever.

There is a rule of thumb that if one machine starts, it will attract three others. Usually around the cocktail hour. Home weary from work, the best thing to do is tackle the grass.

To counter this threat, we have a little fountain on the deck. It won't cut out the noise of mowers completely but it softens what we can hear. At least it makes us feel better.

Soil

Soil is like any other living material: it needs to be protected. When patches of it are left exposed, weeds move right in. It's one way that nature protects this precious resource.

Observe how the human skin functions. It holds the mass of our bodies together, and think how delicate it is, how strong but utterly fragile. The earth's skin is similar. If it's exposed to glaring sun, it bakes, it burns, it will turn to dust. If rain or other repeated activity beats down on it, it will become pure sand.

Soil didn't come to us easily. The earth started out as rock. Billions of years of unceasing weathering eventually formed this tiny bit of crust. As the rock broke down, it supplied nutrients, slowly building up a material that would support life.

Nature has many ways of protecting itself: trees, shrubs, weeds, and grasses all help keep the soil in place. When they are removed, the soil disappears with them. We have only to look at our prairies.

This deep loam took thousands of years after the last great ice age to build to the incredible depth of four feet, and it's taken less than a century to eliminate the best part of that. We removed the natural grasses, eliminated the animals (bison) adapted to them, and grew vast tracts of monocrops. We're doing the same thing when we open up the rain forest for commerce.

When we willingly remove protection from the soil, it's like spiting ourselves and, equally, willing the speed of our destruction.

Attacked by birds

We were summering in a small fishing village on the Bay of Fundy when I ventured close to the edge of the cliffs. Suddenly the whole face seemed to rise up. Sea gulls nesting. They dive-bombed shrieking, whirling, chasing me for at least a mile. This instilled a healthy fear of birds that has never left. Just the sound of wings can cause a primordial *frisson* — I never visit aviaries.

My old cat Mickie used to be able to pick an unwary little bird right out of the air. She'd sort of eat them but mostly she'd pile the bodies up by the back door. And all through her childhood, our daughter, Jennifer, rescued damaged birds, put them in shoe boxes to recover. Always the shoe boxes became caskets. Another funeral, another flood of tears.

The turning point in Mickie's birding career came the day she didn't quite get the bird she'd swiped at. A few tail feathers — just enough to confuse the baby bird who hopped crazily through the nearest dense border. Then I heard the screams of the parents — encouraging the baby back to the nest. Or yelling at Mick.

In spite of the relentless barrage, intrepid old Mickie, the killer restored, stalked her prey. The anguished cries of the parents suddenly turned very ugly. They attacked my cat. A distinct *boink* could be heard as the first beak hit her head.

Mick persisted. *Boink* again, followed by a *boink*, *boink*. Mickie was getting a little confused. Eventually she came slinking back home. As I comforted her my sympathies were all for this old cat. Birds take care of themselves very nicely when they need to.

Cottage sounds

Every year we go to a friend's cottage — with mixed feelings. The friends are wonderful, it is the noise that's frightful. If it weren't for the sound of water moving over the rocks, we could be in the middle of the city. The drone of motorboats, a private plane passing overhead, and the whine of buzzsaws felling unoffending trees make a raucous introduction to the wilderness.

The silence comes only in the early morning just as the sun is coming up. Anna and I go out in the canoe even before the fishermen start gearing up. We slip quickly and quietly into the water without speaking — we've done this so often.

The sound of bullfrogs greet the day; the warning scream of an osprey as we draw too close to a nest perched up on top of a telephone pole; the humble splash of a muskrat.

There are few other sounds than the dipping of the paddles in water. There is no necessity to talk, just to point out a plant or a nest or indicate to go left or right. We pass quietly through a bay created by a huge beaver lodge. We paddle around its island looking for signs of activity, but they've heard us long before we arrived no matter how silently we move.

As we pass through water lilies to get to open water, the noise of speeding motors hits us. The fishermen are racing to get to the best spots to spend a day listening to other motorboats.

All these noises makes me wonder why we have to take our frenzied machines with us wherever we go. Are we still frightened in some primitive way of being alone in the wilderness?

Meadow gardening

Meadows have become fashionable. Especially now that you can buy them in a can. So easy, it says here, just dig up the soil, smooth down and sow these seeds and you'll have a carefree meadow in a few weeks. I tried it. Once.

It doesn't quite work that way of course. Masses of wonderful annuals thrown into the mix came up the first year. This dazzles a tyro. Lots of lovely little poppies and bachelor's buttons not seen in our native meadows. And never seen again here. The second year the true nature of the package was in evidence: tough old oxeye daisies took over.

Many years ago, a friend decided she wanted a meadow outside her country house. She planted madly the first year and loved the effect. By year three there was nothing but Queen Anne's lace, black-eyed Susans, and millions of weeds. Not exactly the effect she had in mind.

Just what is it we think of when we think meadow? Certainly all of these plants as well as yarrow, liatris, cone-flowers, goldenrod, and, of course, native grasses.

Meadows require a certain kind of culture. They have a succession of plants developed over millennia, adapted specifically to certain conditions. A meadow grown on clay will be different from one on sandy soil. Or those in dry and hot, wet and cool climates. Differences in germination times of all meadow plants allow for a natural succession of plant sizes and needs. A real meadow adds not only color and sound but is a whole new way of gardening.

Rules of thumb

I don't like the connotation of a rule of thumb; it was an invention of English law for the size of stick you could beat your wife and children with — nothing larger than your thumb. But it's a phrase that seems apt in the garden. We talk of green and brown thumbs, then why not rules of thumb?

There are some that seem unbreakable to me. For instance, I make great plans for an area of the garden and as soon as I go indoors this space, in my mind's eye, expands to at least twice the real size.

Another of these rules is that if you plant a lot of bulbs and you want to put in a new shrub, you can be sure that you'll hit the bulbs almost dead center and slice them in half. Some actually will survive this non-technique of division.

If you have a carefully composed small picture in one border, you can bet that the new plant, the *coup de grâce*, will be mislabelled. Instead of being blue, it will be bright orangey red.

If you want a new plant to sit comfortably at the front of any newly installed bed, that plant will be the one to grow six feet in a season. Somewhere in the back there is a six-incher pleading for light.

It's a rule of thumb that if you don't look carefully at a shrub for a couple of years, a huge weed tree will grow up through the middle of it. How we can go through the garden and not see this happening is beyond me, but we do. Rules of thumb are not made to be broken, they only come by observation and each garden has its own.

Queen Anne's lace

Before I became a dedicated gardener I saw the world in a very different way. Stuff grew in a variety of colors. Plants appealed or didn't — depending on the mood. But as a gardener, I see subtleties unimagined before. What once looked like weeds are really herbs, or plants escaped from gardens generations ago, or wildflowers of enormous beauty.

Queen Anne's lace is one example. I was trained to see this not as a lovely flower, but as a symbol of neglect — a weed. This was substantiated by seeing it hacked out of roadsides like some invading brute force. Any old feckless grass being preferred.

How could I have known that this plant is in the carrot family (*Daucus carota*) and has long tap roots that draw nutrients lying deep in the soil to the surface? How could I know that this emblem of abandoned places works hard to restore poor soil and protect the land? Or that ladybugs and other such good insects love this plant and will come and live in any garden where it flourishes?

In a cost-cutting measure, roadside verges are no longer mown down. Some people think it looks untidy. But to gardeners it is the thrill of seeing things grow the way nature intended.

These places are no longer dull patches of grass, they are filled with color that changes with every season and are homes for bugs and butterflies. Wild aster and goldenrod spring up to produce a riot of color in the autumn. Who would want to be deprived of this sight? How we've been trained to view nature as children too often keeps us from seeing the genuine beauty of the natural world.

Finale

I don't like to get overwrought about what's good and what's bad in the garden. Small miracles appear constantly. A daily hit of serendipity. Most days such wondrous things go on that my mind churns over on how remarkable this all is.

My garden is my library, my teacher and guide, and it gives me the comfort afforded by little else than a very close and loving family and friends.

Time is my only enemy here. Will there ever be enough time to do everything I want? Some days I despair, others I putter along working with the measured pace that gives me the greatest pleasure of all — losing myself.

The garden has taught me how to be more self-reliant. That I don't need to be surrounded by people all the time to assuage my own loneliness or if I am particularly sad and moody.

It's all here in my microcosm. The beauty I need to sustain a life in the crowded city. The fragrance and textures to keep my sensual life well and truly alive. And comfort to my soul.